Fire Towers of the Catskills

Fire Towers of the Catskills

Their History and Lore

by Martin Podskoch

PURPLE MOUNTAIN PRESS
Fleischmanns, New York

Fire Towers of the Catskills: Their History and Lore

First Edition 2000

Published by
Purple Mountain Press, Ltd.
1060 Main Street, P.O. Box 309
Fleischmanns, New York 12430-0309
914-254-4062
914-254-4476 (fax)
purple@catskill.net
http://www.catskill.net/purple

The author welcomes new information and corrections.
RD 2 Box 78, Delhi, NY 13753   (607) 746-6220
Email: podskoch@dmcom.net.

Library of Congress Cataloging-in-Publication Data

Podskoch, Martin, 1943-
    Fire towers of the Catskills : their history and lore / by Martin Podskoch.-- 1st ed.
      p. cm.
    Includes bibliographical references.
    ISBN 1-930098-10-3 (alk. paper)
     1. Fire lookout stations--New York (State)--Catskill Mountains--History. 2. Fire
lookouts--New York (State)--Catskill Mountains--Anecdotes. I. Title.

SD421.375 .P63 2000
634.9'618'0974738--dc21

                                                                        00-040246

Cover and frontispiece graphic by Tony Sansevero
Cover design by Sallie Way

Manufactured in the United States of America on acid-free paper.

5 4 3 2

Table of Contents

Foreword

THOSE OF US who grew up in the Catskills during the '30s and '40s looked at fire towers on the surrounding hills and mountains as part of the natural landscape. They were like magnets; drawing one's "eyes unto the hills" as it were and daring young boys to climb mountains and explore summits they might otherwise have thought out of reach.

My first sighting of a fire tower (officially called a fire observation station) was from an open meadow near the upper sap bush on our family farm. It was a far piece, as my grandfather would have said--some eight miles away, it marked the top of Hunter Mountain, the highest in the ring of mountains that blocked the end of the Spruceton Valley. Whenever I came that way, I stopped for a few minutes and, sitting on a convenient rock, made plans to reach the tower some day.

In time, I did. During my teen years I hiked there again and again. Occasionally, I went with friends, and we camped overnight in a small clearing just back from the edge of the open cliff that looked out and down the long valley from where we had come. Other times I went alone, wandering all over the mountain eschewing the foot trails where I might meet people who would spoil the solitude I was there for.

On warm spring days, I hitched a ride with the milk truck up to the last farm. From there I walked over the mountain to catch the school bus on the other side--or so my mother thought. If it seemed a good day for important things, I sat in the woods until the bus passed. The day was then mine to hike the trails, seek out hidden glens, wander the streams looking for waterfalls, and glory in the natural world. With an eye on the sun, I gauged when it was time to trek to the school and catch the bus for home. I was sure I succeeded in fooling my mother about how I spent those days. However, she told me years later she knew what I was up to but decided I might learn more in the hills than sitting in a classroom just staring out the window to where I really wanted to be.

In later years, I convinced the girl I was to marry that she should make the climb with me. She did, reluctantly, and wonders to this day how I cooked the hot dogs for our lunch without any butter to grease the frying pan. Nevertheless, she went again when we took our children up that old familiar trail that seemed always to offer something new.

In all those visits to the top of Hunter Mountain, the tower was, of course, the goal. However, it is the men--and women--who staffed this and the other towers that are the reason for treasured memories. Rustics though some may have been, they excelled at public relations far better than all the overpaid, college-educated, politically-motivated spokespersons who now front for the government in Albany and elsewhere. One could always count on the observer for a smile and a hearty welcome to his or her mountain top, a good story or two, a lesson in how to treat the high country and the plants and animals that made it alive.

For all that, my most memorable trip to a fire tower was on another mountain. I had been asked to survey an illusive boundary line that ran up one of the long ridges of Balsam Lake Mountain. Trying to find some sign of it, I climbed higher and higher under a threatening sky. The clouds closed in, and a light rain began to fall. I reached the corner I was seeking well up the mountain in an impenetrable mist. Deciding then to visit the fire tower on the mountain, I set a bearing on my compass, angling to the left where I knew the trail to be. Finally reaching it, I followed along to the top as the murk became even thicker. I almost bumped into the observer's cabin before I realized I was at the summit. When I reached the top landing of the tower, I could see only two levels below. The ground was lost to view. It was as if I was floating all alone above the rest of the world.

From the time of my first visit to the Hunter Mountain fire tower, I set my sights on someday being an observer there. While I had a number of positions in my career with the Conservation Department (as it was known back then), that was one I didn't attain. Obviously, I had aimed too high. However, one of the tasks assigned to me early on was to prepare the maps that centered in each of the Catskill fire towers and provided the means for locating errant smokes that threatened to disrupt the green that blanketed their part of the world. To my chagrin, in my closing years with the department, I presided over the final demise of the fire towers as they gave way to the modern method of aerial detection as the system for spotting forest fires.

How fortunate that concerned individuals and organizations have taken up the challenge of preserving, restoring, and giving a future to the five fire towers that remain standing in the Catskills. We are richer too because Marty Podskoch came along to mine the past and document the history of the towers and, especially, record the memories and images of the people who made them unique. His book is to read, set aside, and then take up again to renew acquaintances and revel in the story of those just plain folks who watched over the countryside we call home.

Norman Van Valkenburgh
Saugerties, New York

Merwin (Mike) Todd, 1877-1960, was an observer on Balsam Lake Mountain for 29 years. A well-known storyteller, he was popular with hikers.
Maggie Stuart Rosa

Introduction

IT ALL BEGAN on a fall weekend in 1988. Merle Loveless and I set out to climb Hunter Mountain. It was my first serious hike in the Catskills, and we were looking forward to the challenge. The sky was battleship grey on the fateful Sunday morning, and I was totally unaware that our adventure would have a profound effect on my life.

We drove to the Becker Hollow parking area, signed the hiking register, and began our ascent. The trail rose gradually at first, but soon the climb became steeper. When we reached the halfway point, it began to snow. At first we enjoyed the sight of the cascading flakes falling quietly in the surrounding forest, but when the leaf-strewn earth was shrouded with snow crystals, our footing became treacherous. The trail grew steeper. I had to grab saplings and trees along the path to pull myself up the mountain. Undaunted, we labored upward for another half hour until we came to level ground. What had started as a challenge had become most uncomfortable. We were cold and wet and tired when saw a cabin with smoke billowing from the chimney, a welcome sight indeed. In front of the cabin was the Hunter Mountain Fire Tower.

When we reached the cabin, the door swung open, and an elderly gentleman beckoned us to come in. We sat on wooden chairs, absorbing the heat from his wood stove. I do not remember the man's name, but he was a first-rate storyteller, regaling us for some time with his memories of working as a fire observer. His stories fascinated us, and I'm sure it was he who planted the seeds of interest that led to this book. He spoke warmly of his daily tasks, of the dangers of forest fires, but mostly of the people he met from all over the world who hiked, as we had, to the Hunter Mountain Tower.

Merle asked if we could climb the tower to get a better view of the countryside. The observer warned that the steps would be slippery because of the snow, but Merle was determined. I, on the other hand, was less enthusiastic, because I suffer from acrophobia

(hardly a promising condition for someone who would soon be reporting on the fire towers of the Catskills).

Nevertheless, I followed Merle gingerly as far as the second landing, and then it hit, that sense of panic that arrived whenever I felt the ground receding beneath my feet. Merle did his best to cajole me to further heights but to no avail. A strong wind had come up; it felt like a mini-hurricane to me as the tower began to sway. I could not wait to set my feet once again on terra firma.

Nine years later in the spring of 1997, I got a call from Wray Rominger, co-publisher of Purple Mountain Press. He remembered me telling him about my interest in preserving the fire towers and desire to save the stories of the people who worked at them. Wray told me that there was a movement in the Catskills to restore the towers and asked if I would give a talk about the history of the fire towers as part of a lecture series at Belleayre Mountain that summer. From this talk I could write a short book about the history of the fire towers of the Catskills.

I readily agreed. How could I go wrong? I loved hiking and history. This allowed me to do both!

* * *

At first I was going to limit my research to the five remaining towers in the Catskill Forest Preserve "Blue Line," but I discovered soon that fire towers in the surrounding foothills and the neighboring Shawangunk Mountains played a role in fire protection for the Catskills. Fire tower observers of the Shawangunks had a clear view of the Catskills, and when they spotted fires there, they communicated with the Catskill tower closest to the blaze and with triangulation fixed the site accurately.

For the purposes of this study of 23 fire towers, I have chosen the broad definition of the Catskills used by Arthur Adams in his book *The Catskills: A Guide to the Mountains and Nearby Valleys*. His "Catskill Region" includes the Shawangunk Mountains, the portion of Orange County west of and including the Shawangunk Mountains, the southern part of Schoharie County, the southeastern corner of Otsego County on the Susquehanna River, in addition to all of Ulster, Delaware, Greene, and Sullivan Counties.

After driving thousands of miles; climbing 23 mountains one or more times; meeting observers, their wives, children and grandchildren; gathering heart-

warming stories and pictures; visiting rangers and foresters; and searching files and reports of New York State, I have a book that will share with you the stories of men and women whose dedication and perseverance helped protect our beautiful Catskill region.

Martin Podskoch
Delhi, New York

Conservation Department Map of New York State Fire Observation Stations

Towers in this book are in bold face. The only tower in operation at the turn of the 21st century is #86, Sterling Mountain. This map is circa 1965.

District 1
1 Bramley Mt.
2 Rock Rift
3 Twadell Point
4 Utsayantha Mt.
5 Hooker Hill
6 Leonard Hill
7 Petersburg Mt.
District 2
8 Ingraham Hill
9 Page Pond Hill
10 Berry Hill
11 Brookfield
12 Georgetown Mt.
District 3
13 Morgan Hill
14 Padlock Hill
District 4

15 Jersey Hill
16 Alma Mt.
17 Sugar Hill
18 Erwin
19 Plattsburgh T.
District 5
20 Hartzfelt Hill
21 McCarty Hill
22 Summit Mt.
District 6
23 Bald Mt.
24 Gomer Hill
25 New Boston
26 Number 4
27 Swancott Hill
28 Castor Hill
District 7
29 Arab Mt.

30 Cat Mt.
31 Catamount Mt.
32 Moosehead Mt.
33 Tooley Pond Mt.
34 White's Hill
District 8
35 Dairy Hill
36 Ft. Noble Mt.
37 Moose River Mt.
38 Stillwater
39 Woodhull Mt.
40 Penn Mt.
41 Rondaxe Mt.
District 9
42 Lyon Mt
43 Palmer Hill
44 Adams Mt
45 Belfry Mt.

46 Boreas Mt.
47 Goodenow Mt.
48 Hurricane Mt
49 Makomis Mt.
50 Pharoah Mt.
51 Pok-O-Moonshine
52 Vanderwhacker
53 Whiteface Mt.
54 Ampersand Mt.
55 Azure
56 De Bar Mt
District 9
57 Loon Lake
58 Mt. Morris
59 St. Regis Mt.
District 10
60 Kane Mt
61 Blue Mt

62 Cathead Mt.
63 Hamilton Mt.
64 Kempshall mt.
65 Owl's Head Mt.
66 Pillsbury Mt.
67 Snowy Mt.
68 T-Lake Mt.
69 Tomany Mt.
70 Wakely Mt.
71 West Mt.
District 11
72 Cornell Hill
73 Hadley Mt.
74 Spruce Mt.
75 Crane Mt.

76 Gore Mt.
77 Prospect Mt.
78 Swede Mt.
79 Black Mt.
80 Colfax
District 12
81 Beebe Hill
82 Hunter Mt.
83 Dickinson Hill
84 No. 7 Hill
District 13
85 Graham
86 Sterling Mt.
87 Jackie Jones T.
88 Chapin Hill

89 Roosa Gap
90 Balsam Lake Mt.
91 Belleayre Mt.
92 High Point
93 Mohonk Mt.
94 Mt. Tremper
95 Overlook Mt.
96 Red Hill
District 14
97 Beacon Mt.
98 Clove Mt.
99 Stissing Mt.
100 Ninham Mt.
101 Cross River Mt.
102 Nelson

Fire Towers in the Catskills: Their History

THE LATE 19TH CENTURY

THROUGHOUT the 19th century, New York's forests were subjected to frequent outbreaks of serious fires. The state legislature was slow to act to remedy the situation while tension built between conservationists and logging interests. Finally in 1885, the state created the Forest Preserve with huge tracts of woodlands designated to remain undeveloped. The Forest Commission was made responsible for creating the means to protect the forests from destructive fires and illegal logging. Toward this end, the commission set up a state-wide system of fire wardens with full authority to enlist help in fighting any fire. Over the years, this system proved inadequate, principally because the staff was too small, but also because there was no provision for fire prevention.

THE EARLY 20TH CENTURY

FIRES RAGED across the forests of New York State during the early 1900s and panicked people in mountain communities. Strong winds carried smoke and ashes that darkened the skies like an eclipse of the sun. Fire wardens and every able-bodied man available fought the fires. Flames surrounded many towns and threatened homes and businesses. Approaching flames forced families to flee, clutching whatever valuables they could carry.

Many animals died during the fires, which occurred during breeding season. Bushels of fish died in the streams from intense heat and from lye that leached into the water from wood ash.[1]

During 1903, 643 fires ravaged 464,000 acres in the Adirondacks and Catskills. The fires spread due to dry weather and high winds. Gusts carried sparks to new locations before fire fighters could extinguish the original fires. Flames consumed huge areas that could not be reached. For seven weeks, from April 20 to June 8, fires burned out of control. Nature, however, came to the rescue when much-needed rain arrived finally in June.[2] The Forest, Fish and Game Commission estimated damage to standing timber in the 1903 Catskill fires at $30,000.

Again in 1908, fires engulfed the state's forests. At the beginning of the year the snowfall was very light, and a drought followed.[3] There were 605 fires in the state, 120 in the Catskills' counties of Delaware, Ulster, Greene and Sullivan. Catskills fires caused $10,669 damage; in the Adirondacks the damage was set at $178,991.[4] More than 368,000 acres burned state-wide.

An exhausted fire fighter.
DEC files

Post-card view of a fire warden by a log cabin.
Edward & Edna Herman Collection

The fires destroyed valuable timber and no new forests grew because the soil was so badly burned.[5]

Edward Hangaman Hall, secretary of the Association for the Protection of the Adirondacks, reported on what he observed after a 1908 fire: "The scene presented was that of a chaos of blackened earth, fire-blasted rocks, charred stumps, dead tree trunks standing and fallen, ruins of houses and debris of various kinds. It was a veritable desert in which every form of life, animal and vegetable, had for a time been completely annihilated. Over much of this region still hung a pall of smoke, some of which was due to smoldering embers and some of which had come from extinct fires and settled in the hollows."[6]

Citizens feared that, without vegetation to hold back the soil, there would be more danger of flooding. City dwellers were alarmed about the loss of clean water for drinking. The thought of losing visits from hunters and vacationers, who brought money into their economies, caused concern in mountain communities. Forest-product industries and big camp owners were alarmed, also.

The great fires of 1908 resulted in strong public demand for protection. In December of that year, James S. Whipple, head of the Forest, Fish and Game Commission (FFGC), set in motion the process by which a new state fire fighting system was created. Instrumental in his recommendations was a letter dated January 26, 1909, from E. E. Ring, Forest Commissioner of Maine, in regard to the nine lookout towers in his state:

> They are a great success and we expect to establish more the coming season. They are connected by telephone to the nearest fire warden and are equipped with a range finder, compass, strong field glasses, and a plan of the surrounding country drawn to a careful scale. With these instruments our wardens have located fires accurately 30 miles distant, notified the wardens, and had them extinguished before they made any great headway. . . . In my opinion, one man located at a station will do more effectual work in discovering and locating fires than a hundred would patrolling. Of course patrols are needed to follow up camping parties, and with a good system of lookout stations and patrols you have got a system for fire protection which is pretty near the thing.[7]

State workers built the first fire tower on Hunter Mountain in 1909. The observer stood on the unprotected upper level.
DEC files

Under new laws passed in the spring of 1909, the old system of fire wardens was replaced by a more professional system of fire patrols, concerned with fire prevention, as well as game protection. Other changes included introducing fire observation towers, regulating railroads and the logging industry and empowering the governor to close the forests when the risk of fire was high.

In 1909, William G. Howard of the FFGC placed high priority on building observation stations from where smoke could be seen quickly over the widest expanse of forest.[8] That year, three observation stations began operating in the Catskills. The state acquired the Balsam Lake Mountain tower, a privately-built tower that protected the Balsam Lake Mountain Hunting Club's land in Ulster County, and a second privately-owned tower on Belleayre Mountain, also in Ulster County. State workers built the third fire tower on the second highest peak in the Catskills, Hunter Mountain (4,040 feet) in Greene County.

In the spring of 1910, a fourth Catskill fire tower was built at Twadell Point in southern Delaware County. Workers built a modified windmill tower at a cost of $307.70. By the end of 1910, there were 20 mountain-top observation stations in New York State: four were in the Catskills and 16 in the Adirondacks.[9]

In 1911, the State Conservation Commission replaced the FFGC. It was responsible for lands and forests, fish and game, and inland waters.

A permanent fire force was set up to protect the forests by legislation passed in 1912. The title of "Fire Patrolman" was upgraded to "Forest Ranger," establishing the dedicated corps of foresters that have for many decades protected our state's forests.[10]

In 1912, the state was divided into five fire districts, each supervised by a district forest ranger. The Catskills were in District 5, which included Delaware, Greene, Ulster and Sullivan Counties. The primary job of the district ranger was to prevent forest fires and to supervise forest rangers. He also approved the paying of all fire bills, which included payments to fire fighters hired by the rangers.[11]

The federal government provided money to states to be used for fire protection. In 1913, the Weeks Law provided $5,000 for use in the Adirondack and Catskill regions. New York State used the money to pay the salaries of 14 fire observers.[12]

The federal government continued to help the state with funds for forest fire protection. In 1925, the Weeks Law was replaced by the Clarke-McNary Law. In 1926, the

Aermotor Co. advertisement in
American Forests **August 1930.**
Jim Ponzio Collection.

federal government contributed $29,391.73 to New York State.[13]

From Wood to Steel

The early wooden towers were constantly in need of repair. In 1916, the state purchased 10 steel towers to replace wooden structures. The height of the new towers ranged from 40 to 70 feet. The state added a six-by-six galvanized iron cab at the top with windows on all four sides to give observers a 360-degree view.[14]

The new steel towers cost about $530 each, which included transportation and the cost of erection. Rangers assembled the towers. Sometimes local lumber companies or timberland owners paid for transporting the towers. In 1917, rangers built a 60-foot steel tower on Hunter Mountain and a 47-foot tower on Mount Tremper.[15] Twadell Point Tower was replaced 1n 1919.[16]

Forest Ranger Albert Tebeau of Owls Head supervised the construction of most of the steel towers.[17]

By 1920, only three observation stations in the state lacked modern steel cabs; one was in the Catskills on Belleayre Mountain.[18]

Observers

Observers served from the first of April until the end of October. Most fires occurred during the spring, when the snow was gone and there were large quantities of dried leaves and grass, and in September or October, ending with fall rains and snow. Periods of drought could extend the period of severe fire danger.

The first observers lived in tents, which proved unsatisfactory in extreme weather conditions.[19] In 1911, the Commission decided to build cabins, and by the end of 1912, rangers had built 32 cabins at 49 observation stations in the state, using rough logs or boards.[20]

When the fire towers began operations in 1909, observers worked about seven months a year. In 1913, they received $60 per month salary plus a $12 allowance for provisions.[21]

Patrolman/rangers supervised observers and fire towers. In 1917, their minimum salary was $70 a month plus expenses. However, expenses could not exceed $5.[22]

The fire observer job was a political appointment given out by the party in power. Sadly, reliable observers sometimes lost their jobs due to a change in political parties.

In 1919, the commission provided new equipment for observers. The state installed a range-finder in each observation tower. A circular map was placed on a table in the center of the cab. The edge of the map featured an azimuth ring, marked off in degrees, and a center pin. The observer sighted along an alidade, or pointer, toward the smoke. From the center of the map to the outside of the circle represented 15 miles. The alidade had one-mile marks scaled to help the observer pinpoint the location of a fire.[23]

New panoramic maps showed not only the valleys and the mountains but also the outline of the terrain as seen from the fire tower. This helped the observer locate fires. A heavy piece of plate glass covered the maps and protected them from wear. Visitors were fascinated by these maps.[24]

* * *

Observation stations became favorite destinations for hikers, and each tower maintained a register for guests to sign. Informative observers told stories about the area and pointed out each mountain. Many were amateur naturalists who could name local plants and talk about the animals they encountered. The observers were great public relations people, stressing the importance of fire safety and preserving the forests.

H. A. Haring wrote in *Our Catskill Mountains* that hikers enjoyed sleeping overnight near fire towers: "To pitch a tent close to the towerman's house gives the camper a feeling of security against the wildlife of the mountains and a certainty of shelter if a bad storm comes." Hikers also enjoyed cups of coffee and the warmth of the observer's cabin when it was cold. In 1921, a total of 30,578 persons signed fire tower registers throughout the state.[25]

Causes

The principle causes of fires during 1903 and 1908 were listed as railroad locomotives, burning brush for agricultural purposes, unattended campfires, smokers, incendiaries.[26] Many fires in 1908 developed along railroad rights-of-way. Loggers left treetops, brush and limbs to dry out near the tracks and in the surrounding woods, ready fuel for any fire. Locomotives spewed sparks from their stacks and live coals flew from their ash pans onto the tinder-strewn landscape.[27]

Facing page clockwise from top right:

The Conservation Department placed fire prevention signs throughout the fire towns (towns within the Catskill Park and the Adirondack Park) and fire districts. *Conservation Commission Report* 1929

Observer Barney Howland in the Overlook Fire Tower in 1951. Barney Howland photo

Alidades and circular maps were used to locate the sources of smoke. DEC files

Worker installing telephone lines. DEC files

Clockwise from left:

Walton S. Persons wearing the new 1926 uniform at Belleayre Mountain. Paul Huth

Joe Stedner checking weather gauges at High Point Fire Tower. George Stedner

Belleyare Moutain Tower. After 1926, a flag meant observer on duty, Shandaken Museum

Conservation Department truck in 1928 displaying fire fighting equipment. *Conservation Department Report* 1928

**Typical steel tower construction: Hunter Mountain.
It took sure-footed horses to drag the steel beams
to the top of the mountain.**
DEC files

THE 1920s

THE 1920S saw the continued improvement of fire
towers from wood to steel. In the spring of 1924,
rangers built a new tower at Chapin Hill (1,430 feet) in
a new fire district in the southern Catskill region. In
order to improve the fire protection of the eastern
section of the Catskills, the Commission built Gallis
Hill Fire Tower (1927) west of Kingston.[28]

Tower Communications

Communicating with local rangers by phone was very
important to the observer. At first, telephone lines to
towers were crude. Rangers and observers strung unin-
sulated wire between glass insulators attached to trees.
The telephone line usually followed the trail to the
tower, but sometimes it went directly to the tower
through the forest. By 1922, improved circuits allowed
the fire-tower line to be connected to long-distance
commercial lines.[29]

Burning Permits

In 1924, the Conservation Commission required citizens to obtain permits if they burned brush or cleared
land in a fire district. Fire wardens and forest rangers
issued these permits. They then notified the fire tower
observer, who would know not to report smoke in the
area of the burn.[30]

In 1926, the commission adopted a uniform to
improve the appearance of the fire protection force and
to promote public recognition of the rangers who
issued permits to burn and forest fire warnings to
people who came into the woods. All district rangers,
forest rangers and observers were required to wear the
official uniform.[31]

During 1926, fire wardens and rangers received 600
Indian tanks. Fire fighters carried these five-gallon galvanized iron tanks on their backs and used a hand pump
to spray water up to 30 feet away.[32]

Weather Stations

In 1925, the commission established weather stations
in the Adirondacks to help predict dangerous fire conditions. The stations, improved the following year,
daily reported: the minimum and maximum tempera-
tures, wind velocity, precipitation, humidity, and wind
direction and velocity. Information was sent by tele-
gram to the U.S. Weather Bureau in Albany. When
dangerous conditions arose, the Albany meteorologist
issued special fire hazard warning forecasts.[33] In spring
1927, the first Catskills weather station operated by the
Conservation Department began reporting from the
village of Fleischmanns.[34]

The danger of fire rises during periods of high wind
and low humidity. When these conditions were present, the commission notified its workers and rangers,
and wardens wouldn't issue burning permits. Radio
stations announced when dangerous conditions existed.

Observers' Cabins

In 1922, the commission adopted a standard design for the observer's cabin. All new cabins had a wood frame, 12 x 16 feet with asphalt-strip shingles on the roof and sides. Eventually all the old cabins were replaced.[35] The following observer cabins in the Catskills were built with the new design: High Point, Twadell Point and Hunter (1924); Belleayre and Chapin Hill (1930); Balsam Lake and Red Hill (1931); and Rock Rift (1936).

The observation tower and paid patrol system of fire prevention in New York proved very effective. In 1926, only one-fiftieth of one per cent of the statewide land in the Forest Preserve was burned.[36]

Causes

During the '20s smokers became the leading cause of fires, while locomotives dropped to second place thanks to closer inspection of the spark arresters on smokestacks and removal of flammable material from railroad rights-of-way. (Railroads in the Adirondacks were forced to burn oil instead of coal during the fire season.[37]) Patrolmen followed coal-burning trains during daylight hours to extinguish fires started by sparks from locomotives.[38]

A fire patrolman following a train near Pine Hill. He watched for fires started by sparks from the smokestacks of Ulster & Delaware locomotives.
Lonnie Gale collection

THE 1930s

A DROUGHT, which began in 1929, continued into the first three years of the 1930s. It was so severe during the spring of 1932 that Governor Herbert H. Lehman signed a proclamation forbidding people entrance to the state's forests and woodlands.[39]

These were Depression years and some people sought to make money picking huckleberries in the Catskills and Shawangunks. Many fires were set by pickers to ensure a good crop the next season because berries thrive on burned ground. Others started fires to be paid fighting them.[40]

New Towers

By 1930, 11 towers protected the Catskill region: Balsam Lake Mountain, Belleayre, High Point, Hunter, Mohonk, Red Hill, Mount Tremper, Twadell Point, Chapin Hill, Gallis Hill and Pocatello. A total of 77 fire towers spanned New York State in 1930.[41] The Conservation Department built two steel towers in the Catskill region. The department replaced the old windmill-type tower on Belleayre Mountain and relocated it to make a larger area visible. The fire district near Middletown in Orange County received a tower on Pocatello Mountain.[42]

The need for more observation towers arose after the state passed a constitutional amendment in 1931 authorizing the purchase of one million acres of submarginal and abandoned farm land for reforestation. One area to be reforested was in Schoharie County, another was in Otsego and western Delaware Counties. The program was to last for 15 years, and the reforested land needed to be protected.[43]

In 1934, the U. S. Forest Service provided funds for nine new fire towers to be constructed in New York State. The Civilian Conservation Corps (see below) built four towers in the Catskill region: Mount Utsayantha (Stamford), Page Pond (Deposit), Gilbert Lake State Park (Laurens) and Hooker Hill (east of Oneonta). These helped to protect reforested areas in the western Catskill region. One other tower was built at Rock Rift, south of Walton.[44]

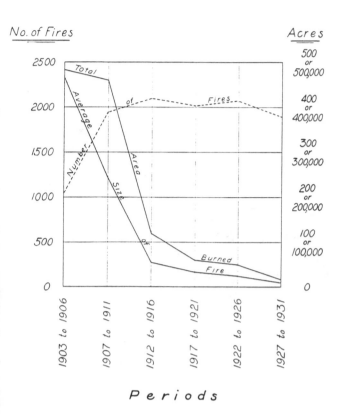

Number and size of fires and total area burned in the Adirondack and Catskill regions 1903-1931.
Annual Report to the Legislature, 1931

New Catskill Weather Station

Because the one Catskill weather station at Fleischmanns proved inadequate for reporting the weather conditions of a wide area, the owners of Mohonk Mountain House permitted the Conservation Department to establish a weather station on their property.[45]

Civilian Conservation Corps

To create jobs during the Great Depression, the federal government formed the Civilian Conservation Corps (CCC) in 1933. This had a tremendous effect on preserving and improving the state's forests. The young men the CCC hired built fire roads, removed slash and flammable material along highways, rebuilt telephone circuits, constructed water holes, built fire towers and suppressed forest fires.[46]

Fire Fighting Procedures

When an observer spotted a fire, he or she notified the local ranger and fire warden(s) by telephone. Sometimes a fire warden arrived before the ranger. The first warden or ranger on the scene divided the fire fighters into teams. Each warden and ranger carried the following equipment to a fire: two Indian tanks, four canvas pails, two fire rakes, two fiber brooms, an axe, and two short handled shovels.[47]

Tower Coverage

To improve its fire protection system, the state initiated a visibility survey in 1938 to see what areas the towers covered and what areas needed towers in the future. Based on a 15-mile radius for each tower, the study's maps showed that observers in the Forest Preserve's 58 fire towers could see 87% of the Preserve lands.[48]

Radio Communication

The southern Catskill region played an important part in the development of radio communications. The Pocatello Fire Tower had its own radio station and was on the air for 510 hours in 1938.[49] The tower became an important center for relaying messages to rangers and pilots. When a pilot saw a fire, he radioed the information to Pocatello. The observer called the

Typical forest fire control truck of the period.
DEC files

19

ranger or district ranger in the Middletown office, who then called fire wardens. This increased efficiency in mobilizing men and equipment for a fire.

Rangers Herb Lepke Sr., Jake Gray and Byron Hill working on road near High Point fire tower.
DEC files

Trail Roads

In 1938, the CCC built hundreds of miles of 12-foot-wide roads (called trail roads) to provide fire fighters quick access to fires. Most had a sub-base covered with gravel and every 1,000 feet a place to pass or turn around.[50] After the CCC constructed trail roads near the High Point Fire Tower and the communities of Cragsmoor and Ellenville, the number of acres destroyed by fire decreased.[51]

Conservation Department rangers and personnel at the Fleischmanns branch office in October 1934.
DEC files

Causes

By the end of the 1930s, careless smokers continued to cause most of the fires.[52] Other causes included brush, grass and refuse burners; and careless campers and hunters.

THE EARLY 1940s AND WORLD WAR II

THE NUMBER OF CCC CAMPS decreased in the '40s but the corps continued to build roads and trails and to maintain observation stations. U.S. entrance into World War II had a severe effect on the fire protection system. The United States granted both rangers and observers deferments from military service, but some resigned to fight in the war. Some CCC workers left for higher-paying jobs in industry. Supplies to maintain the stations were also limited by the war effort.

In 1941, some 2,700 fires in the state destroyed more than 30,000 acres of forest. Even with these high numbers, fewer acres were burned than during the early 1900s. Another serious fire year occurred in 1944 as a result of a long drought, a large quantity of dead vegetation, and a shortage of manpower.[53]

Wood products were important for the war effort, and the government feared an enemy might start forest fires. Sabotage needed to be thwarted. For the first time women filled vacancies as observers, and the work load of both the rangers and observers increased.[54]

In 1943, the federal Office of Civilian Defense created the "Forest Fire Fighters Service." People called it the "Triple-F-S." Almost 20,000 volunteers from age 16 up joined. These young men helped rangers and fire wardens to combat fires in place of those who had gone to fight in the war.[55]

The efficiency of the fire-detection system decreased during the war years. Many observers were inexperienced and could not locate fires accurately, even though they used improved maps. They had difficulty differentiating the type of material burning.[56] Experienced observers could identify dust from a farmer plowing or smoke from a burning dump or a grass fire or a forest fire.

INSTRUCTIONS ON REPORTING THE NEW RED FLASH MESSAGE

The new RED FLASH MESSAGE, which supersedes the Red Flash Message — *Form B*, is designed to give the FIRST FIGHTER COMMAND information concerning the following incidents:

1. THE SIGHTING OF A PARACHUTE OR PARACHUTES.
2. THE LANDING OF AIRBORNE TROOPS (TROOPS DISCHARGED FROM LANDED PLANES).
3. THE DROPPING OF BOMBS (HIGH EXPLOSIVE, INCENDIARY, GAS).
4. THE OCCURRENCE OF AN AIRCRAFT ACCIDENT.
5. THE LANDING OF PLANES AT PLACES OTHER THAN AUTHORIZED AIRFIELDS.
6. THE DROPPING OF ARTICLES FROM PLANES.
7. THE PRESENCE OF A SUBMARINE.
8. SHELLING BY A SUBMARINE OR SURFACE WARSHIP.
9. THE TORPEDOING OR BURNING OF A SHIP.
10. THE PRESENCE OF A LIFEBOAT OR LIFE SAVING RAFT.
11. THE LANDING OF TROOPS AND TYPE OF EQUIPMENT THEY ARE USING, SUCH AS TANKS AND ARTILLERY.
12. THE LANDING OF ALL AIRCRAFT, AT ANY POINT, INCLUDING AUTHORIZED AIRFIELDS DURING AN AIR RAID.
13. THE OCCURRENCE OF ANY SUSPICIOUS OR UNUSUAL INCIDENT WHICH, IN THE JUDGMENT OF THE OBSERVER, INDICATES ENEMY ACTION.

Procedure In Reporting The New Red Flash Message

a. If you have seen, heard or been informed by a reliable and verified source, about any of the incidents above, go to the telephone at the *Observation Post* only, and call the telephone company operator, saying, "RED FLASH." Note that the words used are "RED FLASH" and not the words "ARMY FLASH."

b. After the Army Operator says "ARMY, GO AHEAD PLEASE" you give your message in the order shown on the form below, namely:

1. Observation Post Code Name and Number.
2. The incident involved, including details of incident (brief and concise).
3. Whether the incident was seen or heard, or, if based on reliable information, the details of the source from which it was received.
4. Direction of incident from Observation Post.
5. Distance of incident from Observation Post.

c. Do not hang up until the Army Officer receiving the call says "Thank you" or "That is all," since he may desire to obtain further information or give instructions.

d. If the incident such as the dropping of paratroops involves the presence of airplanes sighted or heard, report these planes by the usual "Army Flash" report before making the "Red Flash" report of the incident. In other words the usual Army Flash Message has precedence over the New Red Flash. IN PHONING THE MESSAGES PUT IN TWO SEPARATE CALLS. BOTH MESSAGES CANNOT BE GIVEN ON THE SAME CALL.

e. In reporting a Red Flash Message be brief and concise, yet complete and follow as closely as possible the form shown below.

Examples of reporting the New Red Flash Message after the Army Operator has said, "ARMY, GO AHEAD PLEASE" follow:

a. "Florence 00; Parachutes; Seen; North; 2 miles."
b. "Harold 00; Burning Ship; Seen, (5 miles off Sandy Hook); S.E; 3 miles."

1.	2.	3.	4.	5.
CODE NAME	INCIDENT AND DETAIL	SOURCE OF INFORMATION	DIRECTION OF INCIDENT FROM O.P.	DISTANCE OF INCIDENT FROM O.P.
ARMY NAME AND NUMBER	SUCH AS PARACHUTES, BOMBS, AIRBORNE TROOPS, ETC.	SEEN, HEARD OR INFORMED. GIVE DETAILS AS TO SOURCE	N NW NE W E SW SE S	MILES

NOTICE: Destroy all previous instructions and forms for reporting a Red Flash Message Form B. The above supersedes all former instructions and forms.

— POST ON YOUR BULLETIN BOARD —

In October 1947, fire observer Obadiah Mulford watched an approaching fire from the High Point Fire Tower. Throughout the day and evening he helped direct fire fighters. On October 26, rangers radioed the Conservation Department plane, "The Goose," and it landed at nearby Lake Awosting, bringing men and equipment. Left to right: Alfred F. Smiley, owner of Minnewaska; Frank Jadwin, District Forester; Edwin Gaiser; two young fire fighters.

Captain Ray Wood photo collection

THE POST-WAR YEARS

AFTER THE WAR, the Conservation Department's lack of equipment and materials hindered its efforts to reconstruct forest fire control facilities. Fire towers, cabins and telephone circuits needed repair or replacement. Trails and bridges had disintegrated. The department began a Postwar Rehabilitation and Improvement Project, but this work was delayed often until 1948 and 1949 because of the shortage of materials, equipment and labor.[57]

New Methods

In 1947, one of the largest fires to strike the Shawangunk Mountains consumed 9,000 acres and threatened the communities of Cragsmoor, Pine Bush and Walker Valley. To help fight the blaze, the Conservation Department used its newly-acquired, two-engine Grumman amphibious airplane nicknamed the "Goose." It could carry men and equipment weighing in excess of one ton.[58]

New Towers

In 1945, Forest Fire Control, a division of the Conservation Department, received $655,000 from the Capital Construction Funds to improve the deteriorating state-wide fire control system. In the Catskills, two new towers went up--Roosa Gap (1948) and Bramley Mountain (1950); four towers were moved--Hunter Mountain (1953), Graham (1948), Leonard Hill (1948) and Overlook Mountain (1950); and two cabins were replaced--Hunter (1950) and Belleayre Mountain (1950).[59]

Improved Weather Stations

Weather stations at Mohonk and High Point collected important weather data. These stations contributed three daily reports to the U. S. Weather Bureau in Albany. Each station took readings at 9 A.M. and 2 and 5 P.M.). Observers calculated the percentage of moisture in the forest fuel, the wind velocity and the amount of precipitation. They studied the condition of the green and cured vegetation and added the days from the last precipitation and the season of the year. A mechanical device using the gathered data provided a forest fire index that helped to predict the danger of forest fires.[60]

Improved Radio Communications

Fire tower observers and rangers increased their use of radio telephones during the 1950s. Fifty-two towers had battery-operated radios. These towers communicated with 66 truck and car mobile units, 42 portable radios in the field and three airplanes.[61]

Fire Tower Safety

A tragedy occurred at the 80-foot Petersburg Fire Tower near Cobleskill. A child crawled under the hand rail of the tower and fell to her death. Proper fencing was called for. Accordingly, in 1957, Conservation workers installed a protective fence of "turkey wire" on stairways and landings. The cost of the fencing was less than $100 per tower.

In a June 23, 1961, memorandum, S. J. Hyde, superintendent of forest fire control, noted that the towers built by the CCC and funded by the federal government appeared to be more dangerous for the public to climb than the Aermotor Co. towers erected by the state. The federally-funded McClintic-Marshall tower stairs ascended diagonally from corner to corner and the landings were smaller. The Conservation Department required that all new fire towers have fencing on stairs and landings.

THE 1960s

DURING THE 1960s, dry weather conditions again fostered fires across the state. In the drought year of 1962, there were 1,532 fires.[62] Governor Nelson Rockefeller closed the state's forest on October 13, 1963, due to the severe drought. A total of 1,429 fires raged in New York State. The following year the forests were closed twice, on July 3 and again on October 17.[63] (See chart page 25.)

During the late 60s, a large influx of people came to the state's forests. Some came for recreation; others to purchase vacation homes. An estimated 2,500,000 people camped annually on state land. This increase caused destruction, pollution and fires.[64]

Forest Ranger Tim Sullivan gives instructions in fighting forest fires to fire wardens and volunteer firemen in the '60s.
Tim Sullivan

Radio Communications

During the 1960s, rangers received a new radio system. FM radio replaced the old AM system that had limited range and excessive background noise. Every ranger received a mobile unit for his truck and a "lunch box" portable radio that could be carried easily in his knapsack. Rangers no longer had to stay near their home phones for messages, giving them freedom to perform tasks in the field.[65]

Fire Wardens and Volunteer Fire Departments Increase

Forest rangers taught at fire warden schools held throughout the state. They trained wardens and local volunteer fire departments in forest fire suppression techniques. Fire observers now had more trained personnel to call when they spotted smoke.[66]

THE 1970s

IN 1970, the Conservation Department's name was changed to the Department of Environmental Conservation (DEC). It continued to supervise forest rangers and observers and be responsible for fire towers.

Air Surveillance

Experiments with aircraft in the U. S. and Canada revealed that air surveillance was very effective at spotting fires and far more economical than maintaining fire towers. The state thus started to close some towers. The DEC said it saved approximately $250,000 a year during the 1970s by reducing the number of fire towers from 102 to 39 and having 23 aerial detection flights.[67]

THE 1980s

THE STATE celebrated the Forest Preserve's 100th birthday in 1985. Ironically, Belleayre Fire Tower was destroyed that year. It had been one of the oldest fire tower sites in the Catskills (1909). Workers using cutting torches quickly dropped the 60-foot tower into a pile of crumpled steel that was used for scrap.[68]

A forest ranger report in 1987 concluded that the public had essentially assumed the jobs of the fire tower observers and aerial surveillance pilots. Now the public was reporting 82% of the forest fires in the state.

The DEC conducted a study in 1987 to determine the efficiency of the state's fire reporting system. From 1982 to 1986, the study showed that only 4% (99 out of 2,383 forest fires) were reported by fire tower observers. The observer program cost about $225,000 a year, but 96% of the fires had been detected by other means, such as local residents and motorists calling in fires. The DEC concluded that, because the towers were no longer effective, they would keep only six to eight of the 31 state fire towers open in 1988.

Many people throughout the state complained about the elimination of the observers and towers. In a May 22, 1989, memorandum, Carl P. Wiedmann, Region 4 forestry manager, stated that the observers and towers were important for communications where

Ranger Ray Wood explains triangulation for a class in 1974
DEC files

radio contact was not possible, public relations, prevention of vandalism and abuse to state land, and helping rangers when the threat of fire was low.

THE 1990s

IN 1990, the fire tower at Red Hill was the last to be closed in the Catskills. Five towers in the Catskill Park and eight towers in the surrounding Catskill region continued to stand. In recent years towers have been damaged by weather, animals and vandalism. The DEC, however, lacked funds to maintain those on state land, and they languished until 1997, when citizen volunteers organized to restore the historic structures.

Catskill region fire tower reports of fires and visitors for 1921*

fire tower	fires reported	visitors registered
Balsam Lake	10	182
Belleaye	13	1,751
High Point	20	171
Hunter	3	350
Mohonk	13	. . .
Red Hill	12	410
Mt. Tremper	9	930
Twadell Pt.	21	252

*The Conservation Commission Report, 1921, p. 124

Catskill Fire Towers Last Staffed in 1970s

Fire tower	Last staffed
Bramley Mountain, Delaware County	1970
Mount Tremper, Ulster County	1971
Mohonk, Ulster County	1971
Petersburg, Schoharie County	1972
Hooker, Schoharie County	1973
Twadell Point, Delaware County	1978
High Point, Ulster County	1978
Chapin Hill, Sullivan County	1978
Roosa Gap, Sullivan County	1978

Causes of Fires in 1962*

causes	no. of fires	acres burned
Burning brush, refuse,etc.	199	1,137
Smokers	184	1,207
Sportsmen	134	641
Children	88	604
Railroads	36	817
Burning buildings	16	72
Incendiary(arson)	12	452
Lightning	11	4
Berry pickers	11	49

*The Conservation Department Report, 1960, p. 39

Catskill Fire Towers Officially Closed in 1980s

Fire tower	Year closed
Belleayre Mountain, Ulster County	1984
Leonard Hill, Schoharie County	1987
Overlook Mountain, Ulster County	1988
Hunter Mountain, Greene County	1988
Balsam Lake Mountain, Ulster County	1988
Graham, Orange County	1988
Rock Rift, Delaware County	1988
Mount Utsayantha, Delaware County	1989

CATSKILL FIRE TOWER RESTORATION PROJECT

IN 1992, George Profous, a newly arrived forester from Long Island, began working in the DEC office in New Paltz. He was assigned the task of writing and updating unit management plans for the Catskill Forest Preserve. In the plans, Profous was asked to make recomendations for the abandoned fire towers at Red Hill, Mount Tremper, Overlook and Balsam Lake.

"When I wrote the unit management plan for the Sundown Wild Forest, which included Red Hill Fire Tower, I wrote that it should be taken down," says Profous. "However, I hoped someone would stand up to save the tower."

In 1996, Helen Budrock moved to the Catskills. "I started working at The Catskill Center for Conservation and Development (CCCD) in Arkville in the summer of 1996," remembers Budrock. "I got a letter from residents of Claryville saying that they were upset with the state's decision to remove the Red Hill Fire Tower. They asked if the Catskill Center could help."

Budrock called Profous and told him of the local interest in saving Red Hill Fire Tower. They met in February 1997 to see what could be done. The Catskill Center wrote letters to those interested in saving fire towers and invited here people from the Adirondacks who had been successful in saving the towers on Hadley Mountain, Poke-O-Moonshine, Goodnow, Mount Arab and Blue Mountain.

"At the meeting it was decided to get a grass-roots committee in each of the five communities to adopt a tower. The Catskill Center and DEC would try to coordinate the groups' efforts," Helen says. This was the birth of the Fire Tower Project.

The DEC requested an engineering study on all five towers before they could be opened to the public. After state engineers completed several studies, local DEC officials decided that $75,000 was needed to repair all the towers. Each committee was given a goal of raising $15,000.

Volunteers organized into the five fire tower committees of Hunter, Woodstock (Overlook), Margaretville, Claryville and Phoenicia. Subsequently the committees met several times at the Catskill Center in Arkville and to discus fund raising and repairs.

Budrock and Profous worked together to design fire tower T-shirts and patches, which were sold to raise funds through the CCCD and the local communities. In June 1998, the two groups organized the Great Catskill Mountain Fire Tower Raffel and Festival, which was graciously hosted by Hunter Mountain Ski Bowl. Businesses throughout the Catskills donated more than 60 prizes, and almost $7,000 was raised from the raffle. All proceeds went to the Fire Tower Project.

By the end of 1998, the restoration project had raised more than $40,000. Through the persistent efforts of the Red Hill Tower Committee, a $10,000 state grant was secured by retiring State Senator Charles D. Cook. Each tower was given $500 by the New York-New Jersey Trail Conference, also. Here is the status of each in 2000:

Red Hill Fire Tower

Concerned citizens in Claryville, fearing the loss of the Red Hill Fire Tower in their community, demanded that the state amend the Sundown Wild Forest unit management plan. The DEC changed the plan, including trail access, parking, restoration and reopening of the tower. Helen Elias led a group of citizens that formed the Red Hill Fire Tower Committee. They raised money through raffles, a well-attended ham dinner, and a letter-writing campaign.

Volunteers wanted to begin work on Red Hill in 1997 but had to find a new route to the summit. The old road passed through private land, and the owner refused access. The DEC, with the help of the New York-New Jersey Trail Conference, built a trail on adjoining state land, and in 1997 volunteers hand carried materials to the tower. The tower was in fairly good condition because it had been maintained until

George Elias and Claudia Swain, members of he Red Hill Fire Tower Committee, removing a diagonal brace in 1999.
Helen Elias

In 1998, Ranger Rick Dearstyne, Dale O'Brien, Ranger Dennis Martin and Forester Paul Trotta re-sided the Hunter Mountain observer's cabin.
Captain Pat Kilpeck, District 4 Regional Ranger

1991. Volunteers replaced and painted the wooden steps and landings and cleaned out the observer's cabin.

In 1998, Trail Conference volunteers removed trees leaning against the tower and shading the landings, causing deterioration.

In 1999, volunteers began removing the diagonal braces one at a time while the Liberty Iron Works Co. made replacements. A State Police helicopter airlifted the new steel to the tower on October 7, 1999. Volunteers from the iron workers' local union in Newburgh will install the braces in 2000, and the roof on the observer's cabin will be repaired and reshingled.

Future projects include repairs to the foundation and porch of the cabin. Once these projects are completed, the state will build a parking area by the entrance to the new hiking trail on Dinch Road. The tower will be reopened to the public on July 15, 2000.

Hunter Fire Tower

During 1997 and 1998, Bo Ripnick chaired a committee of Hunter residents that held fund-raising events such as a benefit dinner, raffle, and a wine-tasting party. They also set up a booth at Hunter Ski Bowl to publicize the restoration project. About $3,000 was raised locally and, combined with state funding, paid for most of the needed repairs at the Hunter Mountain Fire Tower.

Ranger Rick Dearstyne supervised a group of DEC workers who restored the cabin and tower. Forest Fire

Lookout Association (FFLA) members organized by Bob Spear helped at other work parties. Dearstyne says, "In 1997, we cleaned the inside of the observer's cabin and improved the Spruceton truck road. In 1998, we re-sided the exterior walls and completed the improvements on the truck road. In 1999, we repaired the inside walls damaged by porcupines and laid a new cabin floor. We also rebuilt the kitchen cabinets, replaced the furniture and installed a wood stove, new windows, shutters, and a new steel door."

"The tower is almost complete," Spear continues. "We replaced the old stairs, landings, and cab floor. The Summit Shock Facility cut the wood used in the repairs, and a State Police helicopter airlifted the lumber to the summit. Workers repaired a used roof donated by the New Jersey Lookout Association and installed it on the cab. New cab windows will be installed in 2000. The cross braces and bolts need to be replaced, too. We hope to have the Hunter Mountain Tower open for hikers in 2000." (The tower is scheduled to open in fall 2000.)

Balsam Lake Mountain Fire Tower

The Friends of Balsam Lake Fire Tower Committee has sponsored many cultural benefits to raise funds. In 1997, Karen Harris organized a concert featuring Tingstad & Rumbel held at Belleayre Mountain Ski Center, and in 1998 Wendy Nief performed at opera singer Amelita Galli-Curci's former Highmount home. By the end of 1999, the committee had raised more than $17,000.

The eight-person committee, led by Inverna Lockpez, planned on selling stair landings in 2000. Plaques with the donor's name will be attached to the boards.

In 1999, volunteers, AmeriCorps students from SUNY Delhi, supported by the DEC staff, spent several days replacing the wooden stairs and landings. They also installed new fencing on the steps and painted and installed new windows in the cab; a contractor installed a new stainless-steel roof. New cross bracing and bolts will be installed in 2000 with the help of the Wind Energy Power Company of Cragsmoor.

Mount Tremper Fire Tower

The Mount Tremper Fire Tower Committee had a slow start, but picked up momentum when Harry Jameson, owner of the Town Tinker Tube Rental in Phoenicia, became the chairperson in 1999. The committee received a large boost from experienced workers when the FFLA held a working conference in Phoenicia on June 12-13, 1999. The DEC, CCCD, Bob Spear and Harry Jameson organized the conference. The Town of Shandaken donated $500 toward the project.

"The DEC brought all the wood, fencing and bolts to Phoenicia. Volunteers used two ATVs provided by

In June 1999, Mount Tremper Fire Tower Committee and Forest Fire Lookout Association members installed new wooden stairs of the tower. Left to right: Aaron Bennett, Terri Spies, Harry Jameson, Bob Spear.

George Profous

Dan Smith of the Overlook Mountain Fire Tower Restoration Committee works on the tower using a rope and sling.

Dick Voloshen

the DEC to transport materials, tools, and food to the tower," says Harry Jameson. "Local Ranger Patti Rudge and Assistant Ranger Jeremy Burns helped out with the project. About 20 volunteers from five states worked for two days. They replaced two flights of steps. The tower cab floor was replaced and a new hatchway built and secured with a lock. In 2000 the rest of the stairs and landings will be replaced." (Reopening is scheduled for fall 2000.)

"It was wonderful to see workers from all over the Northeast come to Phoenicia to give this enthusiastic grass-roots effort a hand in restoring this historic tower," comments Keith Argo, president of the FFLA.

Overlook Fire Tower

Although the Overlook Mountain Restoration Committee (OMRC) was the last to be formed, its members opened their tower first. Led by chairperson Leo Smith Jr., Sherret Chase, Dick Voloshen and a dozen other volunteers, OMRC collected donations from visiting hikers at the tower, sold polo shirts and set up booths at malls and festivals. The Town of Woodstock donated $1,000.

Volunteers replaced the wooden stairs, the landings and the safety fence, as well as new window panes and floorboards in the cab.

During the summer of 1998, Assistant Ranger Mark St. Claire used the fire tower cabin as his headquarters. He supervised the nearby trails and was an interpretive guide at the tower. Mike Phelps continued the job in 1999, working from Memorial Day to Labor Day.

The OMRC celebrated the opening of the tower to the public on Saturday, June 5, 1999--National Trails Day. DEC Commissioner John P. Cahill, said, "The opening of the fire tower on Overlook Mountain is just one example of the good things that can happen when energetic volunteers work with DEC staff for the benefit of our natural environment and historic facilities. I congratulate everyone involved, and urge them to continue the work now under way to restore Catskill fire towers."

The final tasks of the committee are to rebolt and paint the steelwork of the tower and rebuild the foundation of the observer's cabin, which will one day contain an exhibit on the mountain.

With the continued cooperation of the DEC and the Catskill Fire Tower Restoration Committees, the five towers are scheduled to reopened to the public again in the year 2000. It is hoped that exhibits and summit stewards will follow.

Fire tower restoration promoters: George Profous of the NYSDEC and Helen Budrock of the Catskill Center.
Marty Podskoch

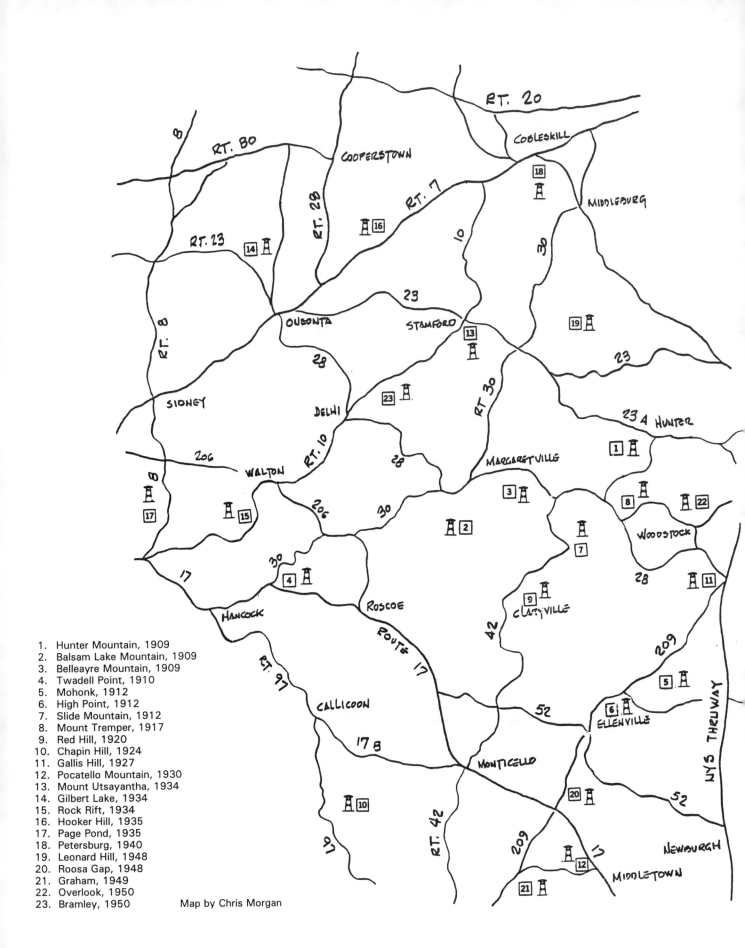

1. Hunter Mountain, 1909
2. Balsam Lake Mountain, 1909
3. Belleayre Mountain, 1909
4. Twadell Point, 1910
5. Mohonk, 1912
6. High Point, 1912
7. Slide Mountain, 1912
8. Mount Tremper, 1917
9. Red Hill, 1920
10. Chapin Hill, 1924
11. Gallis Hill, 1927
12. Pocatello Mountain, 1930
13. Mount Utsayantha, 1934
14. Gilbert Lake, 1934
15. Rock Rift, 1934
16. Hooker Hill, 1935
17. Page Pond, 1935
18. Petersburg, 1940
19. Leonard Hill, 1948
20. Roosa Gap, 1948
21. Graham, 1949
22. Overlook, 1950
23. Bramley, 1950

Map by Chris Morgan

1. Hunter Mountain, 1909

History

AT AN ELEVATION OF 4,040 FEET, Hunter Mountain is the second highest peak in the Catskills. The original name of the mountain, Greenland, was changed in the mid-1800s. It was renamed for John Hunter, a notorious absentee landlord known for squeezing the last penny from his tenants.

Workers from the New York State Forest, Fish and Game Commission built the first fire tower on Hunter Mountain in 1909; the original 40-foot tower was constructed from trees at a cost of $100. For about $50 a month salary, the observer stood on an open platform and lived in a tent; later a wooden cabin was built.

In August 1917, Conservation Commission workers replaced the wooden tower with a 60-foot Aermotor Co. steel tower. Daniel Franklin Mead and others hauled the steel up the dirt road using a horse and wagon. The tower had a seven-by-seven-foot cab to shelter the fire observers. It was equipped with a map, field glasses and a telephone.

"The first site of the tower was not at the highest point of the mountain," says Norman Van Valkenburgh, retired director of the DEC's Division of Lands and Forests. It was about 1,000 feet southeasterly along the summit ridge at an elevation of 4,000 feet. In 1953, it was relocated to the true summit." Conservation workers moved the tower 0.3 miles north to improve the observer's view.

The DEC closed Hunter Mountain Fire Tower in 1989. In 1996 the tower was placed on the Historic Lookout Register, sponsored by the American Resources Group, and in 1997 on the National Register of Historic Places.

Lore

Bill Spencer of Cortland remembers his mother telling stories about when she and her husband, William, lived at the cabin in 1916 and 1917. "Mom said that the

Left: **The first Hunter Mountain Fire Tower was made from three trees. The observer stood on the top platform unprotected from the weather.** *Right:* **Observer Danny Showers stands at the bottom of the steel fire tower on Hunter Mountain about 1934.** DEC files.

porcupines were constantly chewing on the logs of the cabin. She was a crack shot, and when she saw the porcupines through the chinks in the logs, she would grab her gun and shoot them while still in bed."

* * *

Muriel Golden, her sister Inez and their family spent every summer in the Catskills. They climbed the Colonel's Chair trail a few times each summer. "I was the youngest in the group and the kids told me that I was too young to go," remembers Muriel. "The boys led the way and the girls toddled behind. Nobody

Above: **Dan Showers manned the Hunter fire tower from 1933 to 1935.** Leah Wiltse Collection *Right:* **William Spencer Sr. stands in front of the Hunter Mountain observer's cabin in 1917. His wife is seated in the doorway. The old wooden fire tower is visible in the upper right.** Elizabeth Spencer Downing and Bill Spencer

talked to me so I walked ahead of the girls. When I got near the top, the trees were burned, and I took the old trail to the charred wooden tower. I was all alone and spooked. There were dark grey remains of trees that looked like witches' fingers. I was wandering in a ghost-like state when I heard the shouts of the boys in the distance. Finally, I broke through the woods to where the boys were. I was so happy to be saved, and we all gathered near a fire and had a picnic."

* * *

Shirley Wiltse Dunn remembers visiting her uncle Dan Showers, who was the Hunter observer during the 1930s: "I was so small that my grandfather, Oscar Showers, carried me up on his shoulders. At the tower it was a special favor to be taken up to the room where Uncle Dan watched for fires. Granddad pushed up the trap door and we climbed into the small square room

with windows on every side. Then he let down the door so we could walk over it. In the center was a round table with a map naming all the peaks. Except for a stool, field glasses and a telephone, there was nothing else in the room. All around below us, extending into the distance, were the wooded tops of mountains. We looked everywhere for wisps of smoke that signaled a forest fire, but saw none on our visits."

Shirley then went down the tower to the small cabin. It had a stove, a table, shelves and a bed. Her Uncle Dan told her tales of the porcupines gnawing at his cabin and how they chewed his axe handle. She remembers walking down a trail and finding snow under a shaded rock crevice. Snow remained there all summer, and Dan put milk bottles there to keep cool.

"Supplies were a problem for Uncle Dan," remembers Shirley. "But he was a prodigious hiker and was proud of his ability to go up or down the mountain in record time, even with a pack, taking long strides."

Dan Showers later became a forest ranger serving from 1936 to 1965.

Hunter Mountain Fire Tower

Above: left to right: Observer Walter "Casey" Cline stands in front of the cabin. It was covered with wire for protection from troublesome porcupines. Walter Cline Jr. Observer Ernest F. Vredenburgh in 1932. "When I was four years old, I remember visiting him and seeing him in his uniform. He loved hiking and being by himself," says granddaughter Joyce Becker. Joyce Becker **Cline in the cab of the tower, 1960s.** Walter Cline Jr. *Below, left to right:* Observe Bill Byrne and his daughter, Observer Diann "Dee Dee" Byrne Thorpe, in 1997. Ryan Podskoch Observer Hiram "Hypie" Hoyt climbed the steep Beeker Hollow trail to get to the tower. "Sometimes my dad stayed up there for days. He came back down for supplies and to check on the family," says his daughter, Doris Hoyt O'Brien. Doris J. Hoyt O'Brien **Harriet Showers,** small daughter of Observer Daniel Showers posed at the bottom of the tower. Leah Wiltse Collection

Norman Van Valkenburgh remembers hiking from his farm in Spruceton to the Hunter Fire Tower: "When I was about 12 years old, I hiked to the tower two or three times a year. I camped in the trees and visited the tower observers. Their stories were so interesting, I wanted to be like them because I thought their job was so important."

Van Valkenburgh has fond memories of two observers, "Hypie" and "Casey." "Observer Hiram 'Hypie' Hoyt (1943-45) was a great talker," he recalls. "We used to cook hot dogs and sit on the cabin porch listening to his fascinating stories. Later, I took my son's Cub Scout pack to the tower. Observer 'Casey' Cline (1966-67) was the grandest person to talk to these young boys. He showed them how he used the brass alidade on the map table in the tower to pinpoint fires. 'Casey' also told them the importance of fire prevention in the woods. He was a very kind and patient individual."

* * *

Usually observers didn't fight fires, but sometimes their families helped local rangers. "My brother Ron and I volunteered to put out fires," says Merle Cline, Casey's son. "Most of the fires were caused by lightning."

Walter Cline Jr. remembers his father saying that a person couldn't leave a vehicle up there because the porcupines would chew up the tires, the wiring and the brake hoses. The state built a garage near the cabin to protect Cline's jeep.

Ron says, "My Dad used the porcupines to help him. They loved salt, so he would pee on the stumps and the porcupines were like stump busters. The stumps were gone in no time."

* * *

Diann "Dee Dee Byrne Thorpe," the lone female observer at Hunter Mountain, says, "I took the job in 1973 when I was 26 years old. I never knew that I'd have to drive a four-wheel-drive vehicle up a four-mile dirt road to get to work each day. I even took my five-year-old son up with me. We never saw any bears, but it was pretty scary to find clumps of fur on the

telephone poles where the bears were marking their territory."

Observers

A. J. Connolly (1909), Harry Seabring (1911), Walter Dederick (1912-14), George E. Becker Jr. (1915), Samuel S. Styles (1916), William Spencer (1916-17), George W. Butler (1918), George Becker (1919), William L. Lorton (1919-20), George Becker Jr. (1921-24?), Leon B. Furch (1928-31), Ernest Vredenburgh (1932), Daniel O. Showers (1933-35), Warren Newhall (1936-42), Hiram "Hypie" Hoyt (1943-45), Ward Benjamin (1946-48), Hilson Soules (1949-51), Delvern O. Place (1952-54?), Marshall (or Morton?) Francis, Walter "Casey" Cline Sr. (1966-67), J. Durney (1968-72), Diann "Dee Dee" Byrne Thorpe (1973), and Bill Byrne (1974-88).

Rangers

Robert S. Tuttle (1909, 1911-35), Daniel O. Showers (1936-65), Hamilton Topping (1967-77), Rick Dearstyne (1979-).

Directions

During the 1980s, up to 2,500 hikers registered each year at the Hunter Fire Tower. Hikers used several trails to reach the summit. From Route 23A east of the village of Hunter, they took Route 214 south to the Becker Hollow or Devil's Path Trails; from the west they took Route 23A and turned south on Route 42 to West Kill, then east on Spruceton Road for 6.7 miles to the parking area and trailhead where they used the old road to the summit (one way: 3.35 miles). From the south, take Route 28 to Phoenicia and turn north on Route 214 for the Beeker Hollow and Devil's Path Trails or turn north on Route 42 at Shandaken for West Kill. Many others hiked from Hunter Mountain Ski Bowl, or, in the summer when the ski lift was open, they rode up to the Colonel's Chair and walked about one mile to the Spruceton Trail, then about one mile on this trail to the fire tower.

2. Balsam Lake Mountain, 1909

History

IN 1887, the Balsam Lake Club built the first tower on Balsam Lake Mountain to protect its hunting and fishing lands, especially in times of extreme drought. Frank Meade of Arena drew the plans; Sturgis Buckley, the club warden, supervised construction of the log tower. Workers cut trees near the top of the mountain and oxen and horses hauled the logs to the 3,720-foot summit.

Fourteen years later, when six members of the Balsam Lake Club hiked to the tower on August 11, 1901, they were surprised to find the tower destroyed by fire, presumably started by lightning. The club built a second observation tower in 1905, and George Owen supervised the work.

The club staffed the 35-foot log observation tower until 1909 when the New York State Forest, Fish and Game Commission, recognizing the need to protect the western portion of the Catskill Forest Preserve, took over responsibility. State workers repaired the tower at a cost of $38.46. They also added a telephone line and a truck trail. On August 9, 1918, Burr W. Todd transported building materials to the top of Balsam Lake Mountain to build a cabin for the watchman, as early fire observers were called.

Workers replaced the log tower with a 47-1/2-foot steel tower in 1919. This, in turn, was replaced by another steel tower in 1930. Ron DeSilva of Margaretville recalls, "My dad, Frank, helped with the erection of the tower. He worked along with Frank Meade, who supervised the construction." Helping to transport the materials were Mike Todd, Arch Fairbairn, George Stuart, Cy George, Ny Todd, Arnold Graham, Joe Dougherty, George Armstrong and Cy Caniff. Seven horse-drawn wagons carried parts for the tower from Furlow Lodge on the Gould Estate to the summit. They traveled slowly over steep, narrow roads. The material was finally delivered, and the teams made it back at 8 P.M.

The Balsam Lake Mountain Fire Tower closed in 1988.

Left: **These men built the first observation tower in 1887 for the Balsam Lake Club: left to right, Will Haynes, Joe Reis, Dan Hyser, Sturgis Buckley, Jake Samuels, Tony Becker, Aaron Ward, Norwood Samuels, Tony Becker, Aaron Ward, and Philo Ives.** Dot Borden Collection *Right:* **The 35-foot wooden tower built on Balsam Lake Mountain in 1905. The state took over the tower in 1909.** Town of Shandaken Historical Museum

Lore

Merwin "Mike" Todd was legendary for his hunting and his tall tales. He killed some 29 bears and 32 wild cats and captured 29 wild cats. When he wasn't hunting, Mike searched for fires from the Balsam Lake Mountain Fire Tower. Visiting hikers listened avidly to his hunting tales.

Mike once shot a 250-pound bear at the upper end of Millbrook Road. As he walked up to his "kill," the brute snarled, sprang up and pawed at him. The bear's sharp claw snared his shoelace. Swiftly, he shot the bear, and, according to Mike, it was the last time he was so careless.

Lars Avery, remembers going with his dad, Edward, to visit Mike: "My dad was one of the early observers on Balsam Lake Mountain in 1910. He took me to the Balsam Fire Tower to see his friend Mike Todd. I remember sitting by a fire and listening to Mike's hunting stories. Then he would take out some old bear bones and begin playing the 'bones.' He banged the bones together and made music."

Mike Todd worked at Balsam Lake Mountain for 29 years, from the fall of 1918 until September 1947. He had an uncanny ability to describe the exact locations of fires in the Catskills and even as far away as Pennsylvania.

Porcupines drove Todd crazy! They chewed on the floor and walls of his cabin. "The only way to protect the buildings is to kill the pests," said Todd. "I've shot over 900 of them while on the tower to keep 'em from carrying the place away, and I shot many more on the trail."

* * *

Observers often helped in search-and-rescue missions. In July 1968, Larry Baker found three Nassau County Boy Scouts who were lost while hiking. They were huddled by a fire in the lean-to on Balsam Lake Mountain. One year earlier he had found the bodies of a mother, father and their five-month-old girl in the ruins of their plane. That was a sight that the rescuers have tried to forget.

* * *

"It's marvelous for a young family to be united with nature," says Betty Baker, whose husband Larry was an observer. The Baker family joined their father for weekends at the cabin. The children played in the woods and climbed the tower, having the time of their lives.

Baker's daughter, Laurie Moore, says, "I remember visiting Dad at the tower. The kids ran up the stairs, and we had fun tossing paper from the top and seeing whose went the farthest. Then we played in the woods; we were never bored."

In 1970, 398 people signed the visitors' register. Baker always felt sorry for hikers afraid to climb the tower to see the beautiful view.

* * *

Maggie Rosa, the daughter of observer Gus Stewart, says, "I was able to get to the cab of the tower, but when it was time to leave, I was too afraid to go down the stairs. Luckily there was a young seaman who helped me down." Another observer had to blindfold a visiting hiker to get him down.

* * *

Observer Tim Hinkley remembers a young girl and her father who visited him one day: "It was a beautiful day and the two enjoyed the panoramic views. Then a Cooper hawk soared through the sky and landed in a nearby tree, drawing their attention. I thought to myself, 'He looks and sounds very familiar.' Well, it turned out to be Dan Rather from CBS News."

Betty Baker says that Gus Stewart had a sign on his cabin that best sums up the attitude of many of the observers and rangers who worked hard to preserve the Catskill Mountains. The sign read, "This is God's country. Don't burn it down and make it look like hell."

Facing page, clockwise from top left:

Tower in 1913 with Charlie and Lavelle Tait. Dot Borden

Observer Larry Baker with his two daughters on the tower road. He had to use a bulldozer to make the road passable for his four-wheel-drive vehicle. Betty Baker

Observer Gus Stewart with his hunting dog. He manned the tower from 1948 to 1957. Maggie Stewart Rosa

Observer Mike Todd, known for his sharp eye for smoke, served on the tower 29 years . Maggie Stewart Rosa

Observers

Edward Avery (1910), Mike Todd (1919-47), Gus Stewart (1948-57), Larry Baker (1958-1972), Joe Kelly(?), Ken Kittle (1973-88), and Tim Hinkley (1988).

Rangers

Alfred Bell (1909, 1911-12, 1914), Emory Jenkins (1911, 1915-18), Frank DeSilva (1919-21), Richard Borden (1921-25), David Williams (1926-44), Lester Rosa (1944-47), Aaron Van De Bogart (1946-52), Frank Borden (1953-82), Bob Marrone (1983-92), Charles Platt (1993-[2000]).

Directions

There are three main trails to the fire tower. To reach the easiest walking trail, start at Arkville on Route 28 and drive south about six miles up Dry Brook Road. Turn right on Mill Brook Road and go up a steep hill for 2.3 miles. Park at the state parking area on the right. Cross the road and follow the blue trail signs three miles to the tower. A second trail starts from a trailhead parking lot at the end of the road near the entrance to the private Balsam Lake Club at the end of Beaverkill Road. This trail is gradual at first but becomes more strenuous (1.75 miles, 1250' assent) passing two lean-tos near the summit. A third trail begins at Alder Lake on Beaverkill Road in Turnwood: 0.75 miles on the red trail around the lake, then 6 miles on the yellow Mill Brook Ridge Trail. Go left on the red Balsam Lake Trail to the tower.

This is the second steel fire tower built on Balsam Lake Mountain. It has stood overlooking the Beaverkill Valley for 70 years. Summer: Betty Baker; winter: Larry Baker

3. Belleayre Mountain, 1909

Left: **The first Belleayre tower, 1909.** *Right:* **The second tower, photographed in 1949.** Dot Borden

History

IN 1909, the Forest, Fish and Game Commission took over a steel tower on Belleayre Mountain owned by Eugene E. Howe of Griffin Corners (present-day Fleischmanns). It was located west of Pine Hill in Ulster County. Howe's private fire patrol had used the tower to protect the 4,000 acres he owned on Belleayre Mountain. In 1930, the state replaced that tower with a 60-foot steel tower.

The tower was closed in 1984 and taken down the following year. Retired state employee Ed Herman of Roxbury states, "The steel legs of Belleayre Fire Tower were cut down at 12:38 P.M. on March 3, 1985. I remember the exact time because I looked at my watch and wrote it down on a piece of tower that I saved." The tower lay in a crumpled heap of twisted metal. Plans were made for a larger tower to celebrate the Catskill Forest Preserve Centennial that same year, but budget cuts and other fire tower closings killed the idea.

Lore

THE PERSONS FAMILY has a long tradition of working on Belleayre Mountain. Charles Y. Persons was the first state observer in 1909. His grandson, Ralph Persons, remembers, "My grandfather walked up and down from the fire tower. Sometimes he stayed overnight. His salary was about $700 a year. To make more money, he built a cabin behind his house in Pine Hill. He lived in it while he rented his house out to tourists during the summer."

❖ ❖ ❖

C. Y. Persons retired in 1929. His son, Walton, succeeded him and worked until 1941. He then worked for one year at Mohonk's tower near New Paltz.

Paul Huth remembers his mother telling a story about his grandfather, Walton, who was on duty in the fire tower. The sky was exploding with flashes of lightning over Pine Hill as the worried Persons family looked out toward the summit of Belleayre Mountain. Louise Persons waited with her children, Clifford and

The Belleayre fire tower was destroyed in 1985, the 100th anniversary of the founding of the Catskill Preserve. Ed Herman

Ruth, to see if her husband was safe. The family prayed Walton was already down from his post. Louise knew how deadly the tower could be in a storm.

At the fire tower, Walton was just about to get off the phone when lightning struck the telephone line and the headset exploded in his hand. The Bakelite phone casing crashed against his neck and head as if a grenade had exploded. Walton felt excruciating pain. Dazed, he grabbed the circular map table in the center of the cab. He screamed for help, but there was no one on the desolate mountain to hear his cry. He steadied himself and touched the side of his head; he felt blood and heat from his seared skin. He knew he had to get off the tower as soon as possible.

Using his handkerchief to stop the flow of blood, he used his free hand to open the trap door that led to the stairway. The stairs were wet and slippery, and the rain pelted him. Walton quickly descended the tower and rushed to his nearby cabin, where he decided to rest and wait for the storm to abate.

Meanwhile, in the village, Louise Persons called her brother to ask if he would hike up the mountain to check on Walton. When her brother arrived at the house, he reassured her, saying, "Walton has had years of experience up at the tower. I'm sure he's safe." But as he began walking up the trail, he saw Walton staggering toward him, clutching a crimson cloth to the side of his head.

The doctor diagnosed a fractured skull and treated the burns on the side of Walton's neck. For months he could not return to his post. These were Depression years and the family experienced severe financial difficulties, forcing them to sell their home. Walton eventually went back to the tower, but the accident left him very sensitive to light.

"My grandfather would stay at the tower for a week and come home to get supplies," says Paul Huth. He had a wagon that he placed his supplies in and he had a pony named 'Billy' that pulled the wagon to the tower. He also carried lemonade in the wagon and gave it to the visiting hikers."

* * *

Observer Frank Borden, who spotted fires from 1945 to 1953, brought his family to live with him at the fire tower cabin. "Some of our happiest years were when we were the poorest, and those were the years my husband was the fire tower observer on Belleayre," remembers Dot Borden of Pine Hill. Frank had a job working for Bell Helicopters in Buffalo at the comfortable salary of $1,000 a month. He gave it up so that he could be outside and near home, although the pay was only $100 a month.

To start their new life on Belleayre, Borden borrowed a truck to carry the necessary household items, including a crib for their one-year-old daughter, Gale. They put a goat in the truck, too, so the baby would have milk, and started driving up the trail from Pine Hill. The road proved too rocky and they could get only one quarter of the way up.

"We had to admit defeat and take what we could carry and continue on foot. The goat did not take kindly to being dragged up the mountain," recalls Dot.

"When we came into the cabin, I didn't know whether to laugh or cry . . . It had three small rooms. The largest room had a wood stove, two chairs and a small table. The bedroom had a small bed. There was a small pantry that had a trap door in the floor, and we kept our food cold in the ground. I had to swallow the lump in my throat, and face the fact that we wouldn't be walking a few blocks to the movies as we had in Buffalo."

The Bordens had to walk a quarter-mile down the hill to get drinking water at a spring. They carried food, cloth diapers and oil for their lanterns up from town. They collected rain water in a barrel so Dot could wash clothes and diapers.

"We would walk down the three-mile trail in the dark to Pine Hill for an ice cream soda. Of course, by the time we walked back up the mountain, the ice cream soda was only a memory," reminisces Dot.

Facing page, clockwise from top left:

Observer Frank Borden and Verner Tait paint while Lena Tiffany and Karen and Cheryl Borden watch.

Borden (on the left) with his wife Dot, three daughters (Cheryl, Karen and Gale) and Ronnie Tait. Both Dot Borden

Observer Howard Wendler and a Conservation Department 4-wheel-drive vehicle. Howard Wendler

Gale Borden and her mother, Dot, holding a replica of the Belleayre fire tower that Frank Borden made. He was an observer and later a Forest Ranger. Marty Podskoch

At night the Bordens often climbed the tower to look at the lights shining from the fancy resorts, such as the Grand Hotel on Highmount. They could picture the guests dressed in their suits, gowns and furs. "We didn't have many luxuries but we had each other and a beautiful place to raise our children. These were the best years of our life," she says.

Observer Frank Borden in the cab with his phone, binoculars and map
Dot Borden

The Bordens had two more daughters, and decided to live in the village of Pine Hill. The girls often visited their father at the tower and played in the woods. Gale Borden remembers helping her father: "He would put the Indian water tank on my back, and I would help him with the many fires that started along the railroad tracks."

* * *

Observer Howard Wendler and his family also enjoyed working and living at the fire tower. While in the army, Howard met his wife, Lucia, in a small Italian colony in East Africa. In 1960, he took the observation job at Belleayre, and he and Lucia lived at the cabin. Lucia says, "I loved watching pioneer movies while growing up in Africa, so it was an adventure living in the cabin just like the old pioneers. It was fantastic living on the mountain. We didn't have many conveniences but there was so much togetherness. We were in love."

"The cabin had no running water," remembers Wendler from his present-day home in Bozeman, Montana. "We carried our water up the mountain from the Lost Clove trail, a distance of about 1,000 feet, in a large milk can and then put it in an Army lister bag that hung outside our door. The canvas bag kept the water cool. I made three trips a week to keep enough water for drinking and washing. Lucy would carry one side and I would carry the other. We did this in the evening or early morning when it was cool while also carrying our baby, Susan."

The Wendlers had a propane refrigerator because there was no electricity. "One night Lucy and I became very sick and damn near died," said Wendler. "We grabbed Susan, who was in a crib, and we got out of the cabin. I discovered a propane leak in our refrigerator. I shut the propane off and went back in and opened the doors and windows. The gas was heavy and lay near the floor. It affected Lucy and me but not our daughter because her crib was high. We were very lucky to get out alive."

* * *

Ken Haynes was an inventive observer. On one visit to the Belleayre tower, District Ranger Ray Wood found a chaise lounge chair in the cab. It had high legs and faced east. Haynes reclined in the chair and looked out the window toward Route 28 watching for smoke. Wood then noticed an automobile rear-view mirror above the window facing north. He asked Haynes about the mirror.

"You think I got eyes in the back of my head? I got to watch the Dry Brook side too!" replied Haynes.

"So he would sit in that chaise kind of thing, reclining and looking north to Route 28 and south looking through his rear view mirror," chuckles Ray Wood.

During the '60s, the tower register contained the names of more than 4,000 visitors. Observer Wendler says, "On one day in 1968, there were signatures of people from 10 different countries, including Egypt, Poland and Argentina. I looked forward to the hikers and enjoyed telling them stories about the Catskill Mountains."

Observers

Charles Y. Persons (1909-1929), Walton S. Persons (1930-1941), Burlin Chase (1943-1944), Gail Horton (1945), Franklyn R. Borden (1946-1952), William Kenigge (1953-1959?), Howard Wendler (1960-63), and Kenneth Haynes (1964?-1970). Not staffed from 1970 to closing in 1984.

Rangers

Fred Andrews (1909, 1911-15, 1919-41), David Hilson (1919-45), Leon Furch (1942, 45-52), Franklyn Borden (1953-82), and Richard van Laer (1977-85).

Directions

Take Route 28 to Belleayre Mountain Ski Center near Highmount. One can hike up a ski slope to the top or, on Columbus Day weekend in October, ride the chairlift.

Another trail begins near the village of Pine Hill. Take Elm Street to Main Street and go left on Bonnie View Ave. Pass Mill Street and follow Station Road almost to the end. Park on the side of the road and walk to the junction of Mill Street. Turn right and follow the blue trail markers up the hill for about three miles to the summit.

The second steel tower on Belleayre Mountain was erected in 1930. Charles Y. Persons, standing near the new cabin, was the first observer. Dot Borden

4. Twadell Point, 1910

History

NEW YORK STATE FOREST, FISH AND GAME COMmission workers built the first fire tower on Twadell Point Mountain in the spring of 1910. The tower was located near the town of East Branch in southern Delaware County. It was a 45-foot modified windmill structure costing $307.70. A mile-long telephone line was run to the tower.

The first fire tower built on Twadell Point near East Branch. The observer stood on the platform unprotected from the elements.

Forest, Fish and Game Commission *Report*, 1910

"The Twadell Point Fire Tower was first built on the James Allen property in East Branch," says former ranger Walt Teuber of Hancock. The state had a right-of-way through the properties of James Allen, James Hubble and Arthur Twadell. It also had the right to maintain the road and telephone lines to the tower as long as it was in service. The observer reported no fires his first year but reported eight in 1911.

Conservation workers replaced the tower in 1919 with a 47-foot steel Aermotor Co. tower. It was taller and had a cab that protected the observer. Rangers also built a cabin for the observer; this cabin was replaced by a standard cabin in 1924.

The DEC closed the tower in 1978. Today the fire tower and cabin are owned by Mario Genovesi of East Branch. He first bought the mountain; then, when the state stopped staffing the towers because of high costs, relying instead on airplane surveillance, he bought the tower in 1979. He says, "At first I allowed people to hike up there, but they caused too much damage. I'd find windows broken in the cabin and the tower. They even stole the 'two holer' [privy]. I finally had to stop it. It's history, and I don't want it destroyed. I keep the tower and cabin maintained, and I would never tear it down. I want it for my sons and their kids."

Lore

OBSERVER HOWARD "BONY" BOJO lived in the cabin with his wife during the late '30s and '40s. When water in the spring was low, however, they moved back to their home in East Branch. "I would start at seven in the morning and walk at a steady pace climbing the two miles to the tower," says Bojo. "It would take me about an hour to get there. I would stay up there till about six each evening and then walk home. I often walked down from there when it was as dark as could be. It was all in a day's work."

"I had trouble with the porcupines chewing on everything. I kept a club outside the cabin," remembers Bojo. "When I heard them chewing, I'd go outside and hit them on the head with the club.

"One day I heard something outside the cabin, and I figured it was a porcupine. I grabbed the club and walked over in the woods to see what was making the racket. Wow, was I surprised. It was a bear ripping up a log. He looked at me, and I took off for the cabin. I told my wife, 'Come and see the bear.' When we got there he leaped over the nearby farmer's four-foot fence, and that was the end of him."

Being an observer was especially valuable during the Depression. "I was paid $100 a month and that was a lot of money in those days," says Bojo. "There was one job that I refused to do and that was paint the roof of the tower. You had to have a wooden plank hang out the window. One person had to hold the plank down inside the cab while the other person had to stand outside and paint."

At the age of 96, 'Bony' Bojo received a plaque stating that he was one of the three oldest employees in the New York State retirement system

* * *

Gertrude Fitch Horton in her book *Old Delaware County: A Memoir* (Purple Mountain Press, 1993) described going up the wagon trail to the fire tower during the 1920s. "When we got there, everyone was tired and thirsty. The ranger [observer], Mr. Waterman, would let you drink of his water from a container in an underground hole that had a heavy wooden cover. This kept the water pretty cool under the shade of all those trees. You were expected to replace the water that you used and add some extra for the ranger. There was a path to a cold spring about a third of the way down the mountain on the opposite side from the way we walked up."

Horton said, "The boys ran up the tower first to show they were not tired." She became dizzy going up the tower but kept looking up until she reached the trap door. Only two people were allowed in the small cab at a time.

"Mr. Waterman stayed at the tower for a full week [at a time] from spring to fall," continued Horton. "He had a shack there where he slept . . . once a week he

Twadell Point observer from 1935 to 1951, Howard "Bony" Bojo in 1998 at age 96. Marty Podskoch
Inset: **Wearing his observer's uniform.** Roland Bojo

walked to East Branch to buy supplies. He took a bath, changed his clothes and was soon on his way back up the mountain with the groceries and goodies that his wife prepared for him in a pack on his back."

* * *

Berton Bennett of Cadosia remarks, "My father-in-law, Lyndon Early, was an observer on Twadell Point. Children and adults enjoyed visiting the tower and listening to his exciting stories. In his younger days, Lyndon was a log cutter, and he and his partner,

Above, left: Observer Lyndon Early sits on his jeep in 1950. Left to right: Larry, Carol, Yvonne and Berton Bennett, and Clara Houshultz, Verna Early. **Many family picnics were held at the tower.** Berton & Clara Bennett

Above, right: **The cabin and tower, 1950s.** Berton & Clara Bennett

Left: Doug Gregory of Cooks Falls is looking out the tower window. Doug was the observer from 1967 to 1971. Doug Gregory

Norman Emerich, used a two-man saw. They were the best in the area. He was also a great baseball catcher. During the war he patrolled the railroad tunnel at Hawk's Mountain."

Bennett adds, "Most of the fires were caused by sparks from the smoke stacks of the the Erie Railroad and later the O. & W. Railroad. The trains ran along the Delaware River."

* * *

Doug Gregory of Cooks Falls tells about getting the fire tower job at Twadell Point. "I talked to the ranger, and he said that Lyndon Early had retired. They were looking for someone to take over next spring. Ranger Walt Teuber said to go to Stamford and talk to Mr. Carter. Then on the way home, I had to stop and see a politician in Delhi to get acknowledged. I then went on in the spring of 1967."

"At first I used a four-wheeler to get to the tower, and then I had a mountain bike," comments Gregory. "I had a little battery radio that I listened to music on to keep me busy during the day. I had a nice, comfortable swivel chair that I could turn to see in all directions. The view was spectacular. To the south I could see Buckingham Township in Pennsylvania. To the east I could see Tannanah Lake by Roscoe and to the north I could see a little beyond Deposit. I could also see the Rock Rift tower near Walton. I probably reported about six or seven fires a year."

"Many people visited the tower while I was an observer in the '60s," says Doug Gregory, "but the most startling visitors were two military jets. They flew on each side of the tower while I was working, and did they rattle me. God, was I mad at them! They were so close I could see the pilots."

* * *

In 1972, Linda Trask was the last fire observer hired. She also had to get political approval to work. "I had to get signatures from politicians. I sent a letter to State Senator Bush and Judge Terry. They said that it was okay as long as I didn't stay nights. Two rangers were sent to talk me out of the job; they didn't think that I would last a week. But I did."

* * *

"Besides watching for fires, the observers had other tasks," says retired Ranger Ed Hale of Downsville. When there was no danger of fire, the observers were very helpful to the rangers who supervised the towers. They were busy maintaining trails and telephone lines, marking state boundaries and painting the stairs and the tower.

* * *

Forest Ranger Walt Teuber of Hancock remembers doing trail work and maintaining telephone lines. "We had this one worker who was so afraid of the rattlesnakes at Twadell Point that he revved up a chain saw as he walked. He figured it would scare away the snakes."

Forest Ranger Walt Teuber of Hancock worked at fire towers on Long Island before coming to Delaware County in 1961. He supervised the Twadell Point and Rock Rift Fire Towers. Walt Teuber

* * *

Laura Hendricks Rethier, now of Saugerties, N.Y., remembers going to the tower when she was a teenager. "I lived in East Branch in the early '30s and my high school friends and I would sit by the [railroad] bridge going into East Branch," she recalls. "After counting cars someone would say, 'Let's take a hike to the fire tower!' We would pack a lunch and climb the tower. We enjoyed the view and talking with the friendly observer. My friends and I climbed the mountain every Sunday for about 10 years. Sometimes we came across a rattlesnake, and the boys took care of it. The hikes were our excitement in those days."

Observers

John B. Hawk (1910-11), Alfred Waterman (1912-1932), Joseph O. Brown (1933-34), Howard "Bony" Bojo (1935-51), Merton Williams (1952-53), Glenn S. Smith (1953-54), Willis Lyndon Early (1954-67), Doug Gregory (1967-71), Linda Trask (1972-78).

Rangers

L. L. Sornberger (1909, 1911-12), Patrick E. O'Rourke (1913-14), George Realy (1915-31), Leon Johnson (1932-60), Walt Teuber (1961-78).

5. Mohonk, 1912

History

FOUR OBSERVATION TOWERS have stood on Sky Top Mountain on the Lake Mohonk Mountain House property. Located west of New Paltz, the hotel, a National Historic Landmark, has attracted hundreds of thousands of visitors who have enjoyed spectacular vistas of the Shawangunk and Catskill ranges. The first three towers were wooden and built for the use of guests. The last tower, the Albert K. Smiley Memorial, constructed of conglomerate rock, was used both for guests and, for 48 years, as a lookout for state fire observers.

Benjamin H. Matteson, general manager of Mohonk Mountain House, authored a booklet entitled *The Story of Sky Top and Its Four Towers*. It tells how Mohonk was first opened to tourists in 1870 by the Quaker twins, Albert K. and Alfred H. Smiley. According to legend, the name of the hotel is derived from a Delaware Indian word meaning "lake in the sky."

The Smileys built a wooden observation tower on a high point of land that overlooked Mohonk Lake, the hotel and the Wallkill Valley. They named the mountain Sky Top, although, it was originally called Paltz Point. From this tower guests could see six states: New Jersey, New York, Pennsylvania, Connecticut, Vermont and Massachusetts. The 20-foot octagonal tower was anchored to trees with chains, but severe winds destroyed it one month after it was built.

In 1872, the Smileys built a second wooden observation tower. This 25-foot, three-story tower burned on May 10, 1877. A third observation tower, four stories high, was erected in 1878. Guests walked on the top floor's covered balcony or stayed inside where the windows afforded a 360-degree view. On June 1, 1909, however, this observation tower met the same fate as its predecessor. Mohonk's wooden observation towers were never used by New York State as fire lookout stations.

"The state built a fire tower on Lake Mohonk Mountain House property in 1912," says Paul Huth, director of research at the Daniel Smiley Research Center at Mohonk. "It was a joint project of the Mohonk and Minnewaska resorts. The wooden tower was built on a one-acre piece of land we call the Dickey Bar Ridge." It was not on Sky Top Mountain where the hotel's observation towers were built.

Daniel Smiley thinks the tower helped control fires set by berry pickers in the Trapps section of the Shawangunk Mountains. (Because huckleberries thrive in recently scorched ground, pickers frequently set fires to ensure the next year's crop.) "It is believed that this tower was staffed until about 1923, when the fire

Mohonk's second wooden observation tower.
Lake Mohonk Mountain House

48

Left: **The third wooden observation tower on Sky Top was built in 1878.** Lake Mohonk Mountain House *Right:* **Paul Huth, director of research at the Daniel Smiley Research Center at Mohonk, stands by the Albert K. Smiley Memorial observation tower. In 1942, Huth's grandfather was a fire observer for the ConservationDepartment.** Marty Podskoch

observer was transferred from the wooden fire tower to the stone tower on Sky Top," says Huth.

In 1919, the state proposed a steel tower to replace the third wooden tower. The Smiley family and their guests strongly objected to the proposal. A new stone addition to the Mountain House had just been completed and was admired by everyone. To avoid having a steel tower spoil the viewscape, a committee was established to raise money for the construction of a stone tower as a memorial to the late Albert K. Smiley. A Boston architect, Francis F. Allen, designed the tower in keeping with the prevailing Mohonk esthetic.

After more than two years of intense work, stone was removed from a quarry near the site of the tower by means of a derrick powered by teams of horses. According to Matteson, "John Lawrence was a stone mason and it has been said that he personally guided every stone to its final resting place. . . . His son, Frank Lawrence, formed the rough stones using a sledge hammer to break the larger pieces.

Down in the quarry was a steam-operated drill to cut out the stones. It was held by a large tripod and powered by a portable steam boiler. This device required two men, one at the top to keep the bit in the hole while the second man held a water can and constantly poured water into the hole to keep the bit cool." A millstone cutter was employed to put a fine finish on the quarried rock.

The stone tower on Sky Top was completed and dedicated on August 20, 1923, as the Albert K. Smiley Memorial. It cost about $11,000 to build and was staffed by a state fire observer from 1923 to 1971.

Lore

PAUL HUTH RELATES, "The observer walked down for a midday dinner when there wasn't a threat of fire, and he didn't have to work on rainy days. It was a public/private relationship that was unique. Observers were appointed by the Conservation Department but had to be approved by the Smiley family because they wanted someone who would be a good public relations person. It was important to watch out for fires, but the observers also had to keep the visiting hotel guests happy. New York State paid the observer's salary and the Mountain House provided a room and meals."

* * *

One year some 18,000 people signed the register at the top of the tower. Bruce Schoonmaker remembers his father, Grant, working as the observer at the Mohonk tower. "My dad enjoyed working at the Mohonk tower: He had many visitors each day because they were staying at the hotel. Some of the famous people who came to the tower were Jimmy Durante and Norman Rockwell."

Former Forest Ranger Bill Morse remembers how parents enjoyed bringing their children to the observation tower on Sky Top: "We had this fella, Grant Schoonmaker, who just loved talking to the visitors at the tower, and their children enjoyed Grant's stories and his talks about fire safety. Well, one couple brought their children to the tower and the children loved it so much, he let them stay with him for a few hours. This gave the parents a little time to themselves. On their return to the tower, a friendship was built up and the couple gave Grant and his wife a vacation in Florida."

* * *

Carolyn Yantz stood on the stone fire tower looking at the magnificent views of the Shawangunk Mountains. She was one of the youngest woman fire observers in the state. It was almost noon, time for her lunch break. But this was not an ordinary day. It was to be one of the most important days of her life.

A young state forest ranger, Peter Fish, and three men dressed in hiking clothes were walking up the trail to Sky Top on their way to the observation tower. When they reached the summit, they saw the fire tower observer holding a pair of field glasses and looking to the south. They walked into the base of the stone tower and started climbing the stairs. Ranger Fish was a little nervous.

Finally, they reached the 100th step. Peter stood near his good hiking friend, Father Ray Donahue, his college roommate Jim Hawe, and Charley Hurtgam, a fellow ranger.

As the magic moment arrived, Carolyn quickly changed from her tan observer's shirt and jeans into a

Fire observer Carolyn Yantz and Forest Ranger Peter Fish embrace after being married on the Albert K. Smiley Memorial Tower by Father Ray Donahue.

Carolyn Yantz Fish

simple light-green dress. Her three dogs greeted the men at the door. A simple homemade cake sat on the circular map table.

Carolyn walked outside and embraced the visitors. Father Ray took out his prayer book and conducted the marriage ceremony. About 50 visitors from Buffalo saw the union of this beautiful young couple. A procession of spectators walked into the observer's room and feasted on the wedding cake that had been baked by the bride the night before. They cheered after the ceremony and wished the newlyweds well in their new life.

Observers

Frank Duffy (1912), Samuel J. Schoomaker (1913-1921), Matthew Mullen (1922-23), N. R. Osborne (1924-1930), Henry Reed (1931-1942), Walton S. Persons (1942), Charles Lapp (1943-1944), William De Witt (1945), Martin Merritt (1946-48?), Norman Gardner (1950), Harold Hoornbeck (1951-53), Rudolph Siegel (1954-?), Grant Schoonmaker (?), Friend Wilklow (?), Ted Nelson (1967-68), John Van DerMark (1969), Carolyn Yantz (1970-71), and Frank Lyons (1971?).

Rangers

George C. Russell (1912-13), John B. Carver (1915-18), M. E. Terwilliger (1919-1921), Wm. E. Cox (1922-23), Fred Wood (1924-42), John Addis (1943-44), Jacob T. Gray (1945-54), and William Morse (1967-71).

Directions

New Paltz may be reached from Exit 18 of the New York State Thruway. From there it is a six-mile trip to the Lake Mohonk Mountain House: Turn left onto Route 299 and follow Main Street through New Paltz. After going over the Walkill River bridge, turn right at the "Mohonk" sign. Go approximately a quarter of a mile, bear left at the fork and continue up Mountain Rest Road to the Mohonk Gatehouse, on the left side before the road descends.

Those wishing to hike at Mohonk must pay a fee and park at the gatehouse. From there it is about a two-mile hike to the hotel and the base of Sky Top Mountain. From the hotel, hikers can take several scenic trails to the former fire tower, now the observation tower, on Sky Top.

Jack Fagan's book, *Scenes and Walks in the Northern Shawangunks*, gives a good description of the trails at Mohonk. He states that the Sky Top Carriage Road is the most gradual. It begins at Huguenot Drive near the hotel. The road, built in 1895, runs about two miles to the summit. The most direct route, Sky Top Path, begins near the Council House at the beginning of Lake Shore Road. Both trails afford magnificent views.

Many hikers call the hotel (914-255-1000) and make reservations for either breakfast, lunch or dinner. Doing so makes possible a drive to the hotel without the entrance fee of $9 per adult during the week or $12 on the weekend.

A trip to Albert K. Smiley Memorial observation tower on Sky Top provides the hiker with fine views of the Catskill and Shawangunk Mountains.

Observer Grant Schoonmaker watched for fires from the enclosed turret on the Albert K. Smiley Memorial Observation Tower. He spotted many fires on the Shawangunk and Catskill Mountains. Bruce Schoonmaker

6. High Point Fire Tower, 1912

History

HIGH POINT FIRE TOWER was built in response to the many fires that flared in the Shawangunk Mountains near Ellenville in the early twentieth century. In April 1904, a fire starting near the Ellenville zinc mines spread to High Point and destroyed two to three thousand acres.

At a 1908 Ellenville town meeting, the state received verbal permission to use land on High Point to build a fire tower and install a telephone line. The first tower, made in 1912 from trees, had an open platform. Although the High Point tower was in operation for only part of the 1912 season, the observer reported 25 fires.

In 1919, the state built a new 47-foot steel tower on High Point ridge (2,246') in the northern Shawangunk Mountains. "I remember my grandfather, Fred Wood, telling me how he and a Conservation crew brought the steel tower up the mountain on a wagon drawn by horses," recalls Don Wood, the last fire tower observer at High Point. "They reached the summit by using the old Smiley Road. The last 300 yards were too steep, and they had to carry the steel to the ridge,"

The old observer's hut, first built in 1915, was replaced in 1924. In later years, the observers did not live in the cabin but drove to the tower each day, staying overnight only if there was a serious threat of fire.

In 1938, 1,572 visitors signed the guest register at High Point and observer Martin Merritt spotted 23 fires.

During the 1970s, the DEC made an attempt to acquire the one-acre parcel where the tower stood and a right-of-way, but the purchase failed. They closed the

A CCC camp was constructed near the Sam's Point gate in 1939. The young men fought the July forest fire and helped build trail roads.
Ellenville Library and Museum Collection

52

High Point Observation Tower   Sams Point, Cragsmoor, N. Y.

The 47' steel tower built by State Conservation Department workers in 1919. A new cabin was built in 1924.
Irwin Rosenthal Collection

tower in 1971 and transferred observer Wood to the Red Hill tower in Claryville.

The steel tower was taken down by the DEC in 1988. "I saw them slide the cabin down the mountain on skids," remembers John Stanger, a resident of Cragsmoor. "As a young boy and teenager I used to enjoy visiting observer Joe Stedner. I was sad to see the tower and cabin removed."

Today the tower site is owned by the Open Space Institute and the property is supervised by the Nature Conservancy.

Lore

THE TELEPHONE LINE ran three miles from Ellenville to the tower. Ken Wood remembers helping his father, ranger Fred Wood, drill into the bedrock to set the poles: "I rotated the drill, and my dad and ranger

John Addis hit it with sledge hammers. Then they cemented the metal telephone poles into the bedrock. The telephone wire didn't have insulation. They called it 'open wire.'"

"When my brothers and I were old enough, Dad would take us to fight fires," says Ken Wood. "We were paid 35 cents an hour. I hated the warm summer days because my Dad would make me sit home in case there was a fire when I just wanted to go swimming."

"When my father got a phone call at home from the fire tower, he called wardens to fight the fire. He went downtown in Ellenville and got sandwiches and coffee for the men fighting the fire," remembers Jessie Wood Low.

* * *

During the 1930s the Civilian Conservation Corps (CCC) constructed a road from Sam's Point to the

Left: **Forest Ranger Fred Wood (1924-39) playing with his dog. He retired after injuring his eye while fighting a forest fire.** Ken Wood *Right:* **Observer Joe Stedner sits in the fire tower cab atop High Point. One day while he was talking on the phone, lightning struck the telephone wire. A surge of electricity traveled through the wire and burned Joe. The scar can be seen on his left arm.** Mary Lou Stedner

tower. The CCC also put in other trail roads so fire-fighters could reach fires quickly.

During the large fire of July 1939, the state called the CCC boys to fight the blaze. "They camped near the Sam's Point gate," remembers Ken Wood. I drove the Conservation fire truck and loaded it with water at Lake Maratanza. Then I drove it back to load the fire fighters' five-gallon Indian tanks. I worked 105 hours even though I wasn't yet 16."

* * *

During the 1930s, George Stedner, a resident of Cragsmoor and brother of Joe Stedner, grew up near Sam's Point and knew many of the observers at High Point. He recalls, "Martin Merritt [1933-1946] drove a Model A coupe to the tower. He was a serious but friendly man who drove through the gate at Sam's Point to the tower each day. If it was dry and there was a threat of fire, Merritt would stay at the cabin."

Stedner recalls one day when he and his high school friends were watching billowing smoke clouds on the

mountain above Ellenville: "Then Forest Ranger Herb Lepke drove down Main Street and recruited us to fight the fire. We stayed up in the woods for a couple of weeks. They brought us soda, water, coffee and sand-wiches. We slept right there in the woods. We were happy that we didn't have to go to school; we got paid 25 cents an hour. Our faces were darkened as we worked to stop the oncoming fire. The wind swept the flames from one dwarf pitch pine tree to the next. We braced against the searing heat and retreated to find a safer spot to start another back fire. We smelled like smoke and looked like burned logs."

* * *

Retired ranger Herb Lepke Jr. remembers one observer, Obadiah Mulford: "Obie was a real woods-man. At one time he was a real outlaw. He hunted for profit during the Depression. There were others like him who would hunt partridge and deer out of season just to survive. Obadiah later changed his ways and worked for the state as a fire tower observer. He did an excellent job on the tower."

* * *

Observer Joe Stedner knew everybody in the area. He did an excellent job on the radio when problems developed," says Lepke. "His leg was injured in a motorcycle accident, but he could run up the hills and the stairs of the tower when he helped me."

Once Joe Stedner saw an electrical storm in the distance while talking on the phone. "The lightning hit the phone wire at a distance. It traveled right to the tower," says his wife, Mary Lou, "and knocked Joe right across the room. The electricity burned his elbow and cut his ear."

* * *

Because frequent winds buffeted the tower, the state installed guy wires to the surrounding bedrock. Carolyn Fish remembers working at High Point Fire Tower when observer Joe Stedner was sick: "From the cab I had an excellent view of the Catskill Mountains to the northwest. On the east I could see the valley near the Hudson River. But I didn't like being up in that tower. The whole tower shook and moved when it was windy. I liked my stone tower at Mohonk better."

Observers

William Bradford (1912-1914), William Litchrod (1915), William L. Fuller (1916-1918), William E. Cox (1919-1922), George Telks (1923), Eli V. Krom (1924-27), William Bramhall (1928-30), George Mange (1931), C. N. Benedict (1932), Martin Merritt (1933-46), Obadiah Mulford (1947-50), Victor Keogan (1951-?), Joe Stedner (1963-71), Don Wood (1971).

Rangers

George Russell (1912-13), William A. Hasbrouck (1914), John B. Carver (1915-1918), M. E. Terwilliger(1919-23), Fred Wood (1924-39), John Addis (1944), Herb P. Lepke Sr. (1945-66), Peter Fish (1969-74).

Directions

Although the fire tower is gone, hikers can still visit the tower site. Take Route 52 east from Ellenville over the mountain. As the road begins to descend, turn left and go to Cragsmoor. Follow the signs to Sam's Point. Park at the Open Space Institute's parking lot and take the road near the abandoned huckleberry shacks. It is an easy three-mile hike to the base of High Point. Then follow the short, steep path to the ridge. If you stop to pick berries, watch your step. There are rattlesnakes and bears in the area.

7. Slide Mountain, 1912

History

CATSKILLS HISTORIAN ALF EVERS writes that Slide Mountain received its name from a massive rock slide on its northwest slope in the 1830s. Some people did not like the name because it was not dignified and wanted to call it "Thunderhead" or "Lion Mountain." Geographer Arnold Guyot, who proved Slide to be the highest mountain in the Catskills, would not have any part of the new names and "Slide" stuck.[69]

In the late 1870s, James Dutcher, the owner of Panther Mountain boardinghouse at Big Indian, frequently guided his guests to the summit of Slide. To aid in climbing the steeper slopes, he built a trail with stone steps. Tourists stayed overnight at his establishment and began climbing in the morning. Dutcher, wearing a white shirt and tie, pointed out flora and fauna as they made their way through the lush forest.[70]

In 1880, Dutcher built a crude wooden tower at the summit. Guests climbed steps to a platform for a panoramic view of the Catskills. A story relates that Dutcher provided musicians for a night of dancing at the summit. Sometimes hikers camped overnight, and Dutcher entertained them with bear stories. After descending the mountain, he invited his guests to a trout dinner at his home.[71]

In 1886, Forest Commissioner Townsend Cox and a group of officials climbed Slide. They came to designate the Catskills as part of the State Forest Preserve. Cox extolled the virtues of the region's forest and the importance of protecting the streams that were born on Slide. Alf Evers writes that, as Cox stood on the wooden tower, he declared the view as good as any in the Adirondacks.[72]

Naturalist John Burroughs was a frequent hiker to the summit. In 1923, the Winnisook Club placed a memorial plaque on the summit rock. Its inscription states, "In Memoriam, John Burroughs who, in his early writings introduced Slide Mountain to the World. He made many visits to this peak and slept several

Top: The 1912 fire tower atop Slide Mountain.
Town of Shandaken Historical Museum

Another log observation tower on Slide, date unkown.
Ed and Edna Herman Collection

In the summer of 1936, these Conservation workers built the steel tower on Slide Mountain. It was used only by hikers as an observation tower. Left to right, Wallace Andrews (Superintendent of Ulster County Schools), David Hilson (Phoencia Forest Ranger), Mike Todd (Balsam Lake Mountain observer), D. T. Williams (Union Grove Forest Ranger), Gideon Gregory, William Smith (Mt. Tremper observer), Fred Andrews (Big Indian Forest Ranger). Charles Andrews is down in front. Dot Borden Collection

nights beneath this rock. This region is the scene of many of his essays. Here the works of man dwindle in the Heart of the Southern Catskills." Burroughs' stories about the beauty of the Catskills and Slide Mountain are a treasured part of American literature.

Tourists flocked to the area and the Forest Commission allocated funds to construct a trail to the summit of Slide in 1891.

The Conservation Commission built a wooden fire tower and observer's cabin on Slide in 1911, and Forest Ranger Joseph Johnston of Chichester supervised the tower. Eben Chase was the first and last observer because the state closed the tower the following year.[73]

"The tower on Slide was probably abandoned because it was often too foggy at that height. There were other towers, such as Mount Tremper and Belleayre, that had good views of the area," says District Ranger Ray Wood of New Paltz.

In his book, *Our Catskill Mountains* (1931), H. A. Haring wrote, "At the present time Slide Mt. has no observatory tower although one has been promised by the State of New York and the steel has lain for six years on the top, partially erected. . . ."[74]

Thousands of people have hiked Slide Mountain because of its beauty and the fact that it is the highest mountain in the Catskills. Because the summit was heavily forested, the state decided to give the hikers a better view. In 1936, the Conservation Department put up a steel observation tower for hikers. The tower had originally been purchased for use in the Adirondacks; however, at 47 feet, it was too short.

Over the years, the steel tower enabled many hikers a panoramic view of the Catskills. In later years, however, vandals took the wooden steps for campfires and riddled the steel cab with bullet holes.

In August 1968, Conservation workers dismantled the observation tower on Slide Mountain because it was no longer safe. Ranger Aaron Van De Bogart and fire tower observers Larry Baker, John Baldwin, Joe Kelly and Harry Baldwin took two days to complete the job.

Dot Borden Collection

Lore

T. MORRIS LONGSTRETH wrote in his book, *The Catskills,* that he followed a blazed trail in 1917 upon which "there were no footprints." Along the pristine trail he saw telephone poles and wire that ran to the tower.

One long-time hiker of the Catskills, Father Ray Donahue of Downsville, recalls finding a glass insulator while climbing Slide, surely a relic of the early telephone line.

* * *

In 1998, the DEC published its "Slide Mountain Wilderness Plan." To discourage overuse, there will never be any towers on the summit.

Patti Rudge, Forest Ranger for the Slide Mountain area, has been energetic in her efforts to preserve it as wilderness. Many people feel that it is important to put back an observation tower for hikers to see beyond the trees. On the other hand, Patti feels, "It is important to have a place where people can hike and enjoy the forests. A hiker can look inward and doesn't always have to look above the trees."

Alf Evers lauded the proposal to designate Slide Mountain as a wilderness area: "Friends of Slide wel-

come the proposal for they know that the balsam-scented, storm-wracked mountain has always been wild at heart. It has resisted efforts to tame it, it has hurled down tower after tower from its summit, it has wiped out trails with rock slides and floods. It almost seems. . .the shy, shaggy mountain will remain for always a true King of the Wilderness." [75]

Directions

The easiest way to hike to the summit of Slide Mountain from Ulster County is to take Route 28 to Big Indian, then Ulster County Route 47 south (Slide Mountain Road) for 8.4 miles. You will pass the Giant Ledge trailhead and Winnisook Lodge. Drive another mile, watching for the Slide Mountain trailhead in a parking area on the left. From Sullivan County, begin at Livingston Manor (Exit 96 of Route 17); take Sullivan County Route 81 (it becomes Route 82 and, in Ulster County, Route 47) past the Frost Valley YMCA about 4.5 miles to the parking area and trailhead on the right.

8. Mount Tremper, 1917

History

THE NEW YORK STATE CONSERVATION COMMIS-
sion chose Mount Tremper (2,740 feet) as the site
of its eighth tower in the Catskill region. Barbara
McMartin and Peter Kick state in their book, *Fifty
Hikes in the Hudson Valley*, that the fire tower was built
"to replace the one on Slide, after the Mount Tremper
tract was acquired between 1906 and 1910."[76] In 1917,
rangers built the 47-foot steel tower and cabin near
Phoenicia. This site was chosen because it overlooked

large portions of the Forest Preserve that had not been
visible from the Belleayre or Hunter Mountain towers.

In his first year as observer, 1917, William Smith
reported six fires and 17 the following year. During his
last year at the tower, 1930, he reported 30 fires.

Many hikers visited Smith. For example, 930
visitors signed his register in 1921 and in 1928, 1,016.
The Conservation Department built a new cabin for
observer Smith in 1929.

The Mount Tremper Fire Tower was closed in
1971 when the state decided it could save money by
relying on airplane surveillance.

**William Smith, observer (1917-30) at Mount Tremper Fire Tower,
is on the right by the observer's cabin with a visiting hunter.**
Lonnie Gale postcard collection

Above: **The tower before 1920.** Craig Woodworth

Left, top: **DeForrest "Bud" Smith holding a picture of his grandfather, observer William Smith.** Marty Podskoch

Left: **Harry Baldwin was the observer at Mt. Tremper for 24 years. He had a great fear rattlesnakes.** John and Harry Baldwin Jr.

Lore

DE FORREST "BUD" SMITH of Woodland Valley can picture his grandfather, William Smith, walking on the trail: "A lantern flickered on the Mt. Tremper trail as Grandpa made his way down the serpentine path that took him to his wife and family. He'd spend a week watching over the Catskill Mountains for fires," says Bud, "and then come home for a day."

"My cousin, Hal, and I loved to go up to Grandpa's observer's cabin and listen to his stories," says Bud. "He always boasted to us that he never lost a day's work in his 19 years at the tower.

"One day while Grandpa was picking blueberries near the tower, he saw something move in the patch. It was a bear, standing and eating berries. Grandpa decided he wasn't going to argue with a bear. He had enough berries anyway, so he left."

The mountain harbored many rattlesnakes in its ledges and stone quarry. "If anybody came up there to do anything to the snakes," Bud Smith says, "my grandpa would raise holy heck. His claim was that the snakes kept all the mice and chipmunks out of his cabin so he didn't have to worry about their chewing up his supplies or his having to clean up their messes."

* * *

Another fire tower observer, Harry Baldwin, got the Mount Tremper job in 1946. He climbed to the tower each day from his house in Willow. A neighbor, Roy Van Wagner, recalls that Baldwin was exceptionally dedicated to his work. "In fire season, Harry would stay up there all night. We looked at the tower with binoculars, and sometimes we could see him silhouetted through the window."

Baldwin developed a terrible rash soon after taking the job. He had no idea what was causing it until someone in town suggested he use a four-wheel-drive vehicle to get to work. He followed that advice and miraculously the rash disappeared. It turned out Baldwin had a tremendous fear of rattlesnakes, and every day he climbed the mountain on foot he was afraid that his next step would be on a snake. His fear had induced the rash.

"Harry Baldwin would stop at our store practically every day on his way to the tower. He had an old Army jeep, and he was always very happy," remembers Van Wagner. "Harry would go up about nine o'clock and come back about seven, often with a fishing pole sticking out of his open jeep and whistling away happily. Sometimes he'd stop and play horseshoes."

* * *

Leroy Winchell remembers evenings sitting in his back yard in Phoenicia: "We used to watch the lights of Harry Baldwin's jeep as it zigged its way down the mountain after he was done working at the tower."

Baldwin's son, John ("Sonny"), was different from his dad in that he loved to catch rattlesnakes. "One day I was riding with my dad and ranger Aaron Van De Bogart up to Mount Tremper. We asked my dad to stop at the quarry. I took a burlap bag with me and put some branches in it. When we got back to my dad's jeep, the bag kept expanding and moving. We tried to get into the jeep but my dad shouted, 'You're not bringing those snakes into my jeep. You're going to have to put them on a long stick and hang them outside!'

"When we got to the top, we told him that there was nothing in the bag, but he wouldn't believe us. He went inside the cabin, and I threw the branches over the cliff. When I called my father out, he saw the empty bag and said, 'Now they've gotten away, and I'm going to have more snakes!'"

As Harry got older, John occasionally filled in for his dad at the tower and eventually became the observer on Overlook Mountain for 17 years.

* * *

Phoenicia resident Lonnie Gale recalls: "One time, while I was hiking up Mount Tremper with some friends, the weather turned bad when we were half way up. We continued walking, and when we got to the top, the snow was up to our knees. My friends and I were exhausted and made our way to the fire tower cabin. We broke in and started a fire to get warm. We used some of Harry Baldwin's provisions. When we were rested, we left Harry a note that said we were sorry that we used some of his beans and soup. His cabin helped save our lives."

Gale and his friends needn't have worried about the food. Baldwin, a big man at 6'1' and well over 300

Will Smith (with vest) and George Woodworth.
Craig Woodworth Collection

**A forest ranger, possibly David Hilson (1919-45)
of Phoenicia, standing at the base of tower.**
Lonnie Gale collection

pounds, "loved to cook and have everybody eat what he cooked, too," says John Baldwin.

Observers

William Smith (1917-30), Roy Erickson (1931-45), Harry Baldwin (1946-70).

Rangers

Jay H. Simpson (1915-18), David Hilson (1919-1945), Aaron Van De Bogart (1942, 1945-71).

Directions

The main trail to the summit of Mount Tremper and the fire tower is an old jeep road which begins 1.3 miles east of Phoenicia on Old Route 28 (also called Old Plank Road and County Route 40) along Esopus Creek. The trailhead parking area is about a quarter-mile farther east. A trail connects with the old road which will lead you on a two-and-a-half-mile trek that zig-zags to the summit. There are two lean-tos on the way to the summit: one is halfway up; the other, near the tower (slated to be moved farther from the trail and the tower in the future).

A second trail begins on the opposite side of Mount Tremper. It can be reached by taking Route 212 to Willow. From the garage in Willow, take Van Wagner Road to Jessup Road. Turn left and go 0.8 mile. Future parking is planned, but in 2000 there is inadequate parking at the trailhead, so you may have to park along the road about a half-mile before a sign that says "private road." It is best to ask homeowners for permission if you park near a dwelling. Or you can park at the post office and walk an extral mile. This 3.2-mile trail leads to a saddle between two mountains. The trail to the Mount Tremper tower goes left. Watch for the trail markers.

9. Red Hill, 1920

History

IN 1919, the Conservation Commission reported that a considerable amount of forest in the southern Catskills was inadequately protected by observation stations. To remedy this, the state chose Red Hill in the town of Denning near Claryville as the site of a new fire tower. In 1920, Conservation workers built a 60-foot steel tower atop the 2,990-foot mountain in Ulster County.[77]

"My great-great uncle, Forest Ranger Fred Wood, took the steel fire tower up to Red Hill in a horse-drawn wagon early in 1920," comments former observer Don Wood. By midsummer, workers had built a road and strung a three-mile telephone line to the tower. Rangers also built a cabin for the observer. Observers drew water from a spring at the base of a cliff to the west and downhill from the tower. A new observer's cabin was built in 1931.

Observer Elmer Schulz reported three fires during the 1920 season. In 1921, 410 visitors signed the register and 12 fires were reported.

The DEC closed the tower for a short while in 1971, but Ranger Peter Fish fought to have it reopened because of communication problems in the southern part of the Catskills. In 1972, observer Don Wood moved from the High Point Tower to the Red Hill Tower and remained there until the tower was closed in 1990. Red Hill was the last fire tower closed in the Catskills.

Lore

RETIRED DENNING SUPERVISOR HAROLD VAN Aken remembers going to the nearby Red Hill Fire Tower when he was young: "Elmer [Schultz] was the first observer, and he was a nice, pleasant man. He kept a few cows on his farm. When he left the tower, he was the superintendent of the Town of Denning."

Red Hill Fire Tower near Claryville.
Captain Ray Wood collection

Van Aken also says, "My uncle, Ed Lewis, was the observer at Red Hill from 1938 to 1958. He loved nature and his tower job. Rangers told me that he was very accurate in sending them to a fire. We used to go up to the tower once or twice a year to have a family picnic. We drove up the road through the Dibble farm. Mr. Dibble didn't mind the traffic through his farm because often visitors would stop and buy some potatoes or a lamb. On their way back from the tower, the lamb would be butchered and ready to go."

* * *

"My husband loved his job and was very dedicated," says Suzie De Pew of her husband, Claude. "He worked at the tower from 1958 to 1966. Sometimes Claude would stay at the tower all night during a fire."

"He loved hunting and fishing," adds his daughter Caroline Harris. "Dad always said he wanted to die with a gun on his back, and he died in the woods rabbit hunting. He got his wish."

"He loved to play jokes and he loved hunting," says Claude's neighbor, Floyd Van Wagner of Sundown. "When he was logging, a branch landed on his foot and crushed it. They had to amputate it and he had a wooden foot. Fortunately, he was able to get the tower job."

* * *

Ranger Herb Lepke Jr., who supervised the Red Hill tower, says, "We had a report of a lost child in the woods. After a long search, I was lucky to find him. It was one of the best moments in my life when I handed the missing boy to his parents. I'll never forget it."

From his boyhood, Reavis "Sam" Sennett of Liberty had wanted to be a fire tower observer. "After working for the O. & W Railroad, Sam applied for a job with the Conservation Department, and he got the fire tower observer job on Red Hill," recalls his wife, Florence. "He could hardly wait to go to work in the morning. He loved the oudoors."

Observer Ed Lewis (left) with a hunting friend in front of Red Hill Fire Tower garage. Harold Van Aken

Observer Claude De Pew (1958-66) in the Red Hill Fire Tower. Suzie De Pew

Sam never lived in the cabin but drove there each day from Liberty. On weekends he took his wife and children to the tower. Florence says, "I enjoyed meeting all the hikers. They came from all parts of the world."

* * *

One day while Don Wood sat in the Red Hill Fire Tower, ominous dark clouds began shrouding the mountains. Then lightning bolts shattered the sky. Don grabbed the microphone and signed out on the tower radio, "Red Hill tower out of service due to thunder storm." (The DEC advised observers to leave their towers during electrical storms because the tower could act as a lightning rod.)

In a flash Don was out the trap door, down the tower stairs and into his cabin. Don sat at the table and watched the skies get darker. His phone rang; it was observer Ken Kittle atop Balsam Lake Mountain. "What are you doing signing out? It's not bad here," said Kittle.

At that moment, a lightning bolt struck near Don's tower. A surge of electricity came through the telephone. It flew from his hand, and he was thrown from his chair. "I'll never go near a telephone during an electrical storm again," groans Don as he recalls his burned lip and the shock to his ear.

Most of the time it was peaceful being in the tower. "On a clear day I could see five states, from the Berkshires of Massachusetts to the Poconos in Pennsylvania," says Wood.

Don is a true mountain man. His father was a logger and at age four Don was in the woods helping his dad. He learned to hunt, fish and trap. When he got older, he worked at various farms. In 1971, he became the observer at the High Point Fire Tower. When that tower closed, the DEC moved him to Red Hill. Don replaced Reavis Sennett.

Don says he was never bored. "I was busy watching for smoke or listening to the communications radio. I also loved carving spoons, forks and bowls. My other

Observer Reavis "Sam" Sennett and Forest Ranger Tony Lenkiewicz, 1968. Dot Borden

Observer Don Wood enjoys carving a wooden spoons. Marty Podskoch

Many times Don Wood got stuck in the snow on his way to the Red Hill Fire Tower.
Don Wood

job was to maintain the trail and telephone line. Sometimes I would help mark the boundaries on state land when it was wet, and there wasn't a threat of fire."

Wood lived in Sundown and occasionally stayed at the cabin. It had no electricity, so he used a propane lantern and candles for light. He kept the wood stove going for warmth and cooking. "I cooked deer meat and smoked the trout I caught in the nearby streams," he recalls. "During the spring I gathered wild leeks."

Sometimes Wood had to get to the tower after a snowstorm. He says, "I got stuck plenty of times. Even though I had a state military power wagon, I got stuck in drifts that were five feet deep. I had to use a winch to pull myself out."

Observers

Elmer Schulz (1920-?), Ed Lewis (1938-1958), Claude De Pew (1958-1966), Reavis "Sam" Sennett (1967-70), Don Wood (1972-90).

Rangers

W. J. Morrisey (1923-47), Bernard "Bun" O'Neil (1948-57), Herb Lepke Jr.(1957-68), Peter Fish (1969-73), James Kesel (1975-77), Hilda Webb (1977-79), Andy Jacob (1979-86), Steve Ovitt (1986-88), Bob Zureck (1988-90).

Directions

From Ellenville: Take Route 55 (west) along the Rondout Reservoir. Before reaching Grahamsville, turn right onto County Route 153 North. Turn left onto Sugar Loaf Road, then after several miles, make a sharp left on Red Hill Road. Go right onto Dinch Road (formerly Coons Road) and drive one mile. The trail begins on the left, where a parking lot is proposed. The hike to the tower is 1.1 mile.

From Claryville: Take County Route 19 west to Red Hill Road. Drive about three miles on Red Hill Road and turn left onto Dinch Road. It is about a mile to the trailhead on your left.

From Liberty: Take Route 55 to County Route 19 before Grahamsiville or Route 153 after Grahamsville.

10. Chapin Hill, 1924

History

IN 1891, Chester Chapin Jr. began purchasing land in southern Sullivan County. He envisioned a hunting preserve. Over the years, he amassed about 18,000 acres, which he called Chapin Park.

According to the booklet, "Elk Lodge," written by Judith Brewster Johnson and researched by local historian Peter Osborne, Chapin's father was the president of the Boston and Albany Railroad and the New York, New Haven & Hartford Railroad, and a director of the New York Central Railroad. Chester Jr., an heir to his father's vast fortune, made his own fortune in steamboat and railroad transportation.

In 1898, Chapin built Elk Lodge, a building similar in size to the famous Adirondack "great camps." He started a farm and raised enough animals and crops to make the estate self-sufficient. Over the years his large herd of deer and elk thrived. Chapin built a fence to keep the animals in and intruders out.

On May 23, 1924, Chapin's heirs, Elizabeth J. Chapin, Pauline Chapin Hodges and Edward Kelly signed an agreement granting New York State the right to build a fire tower and telephone system on the Chapin estate. Chapin Hill (1,430 feet) was chosen as the site of the tower because of its view of southern Sullivan County. The state built a 60-foot steel tower in the late spring of 1924. It cost $1,500 and was funded by the Sullivan County Board of Supervisors. The observer reported 24 fires the first year.

The Conservation Department also built a cabin costing $400. It was replaced in 1930 and again in 1942 due to forest fires.

During the spring of 1941, when Bernie "Bun" O'Neill was the observer at Chapin Hill, a fire swept the tower site and destroyed the cabin. It also burned the first three wooden landings and stairs on the tower. To protect it, the state removed nearby trees and built a circular fire lane around the tower and new cabin.

Chapin Hill Fire Tower was closed in 1970, and the DEC took it down in 1988. The tower site is presently owned by Orange & Rockland Utilities and is closed to the public.

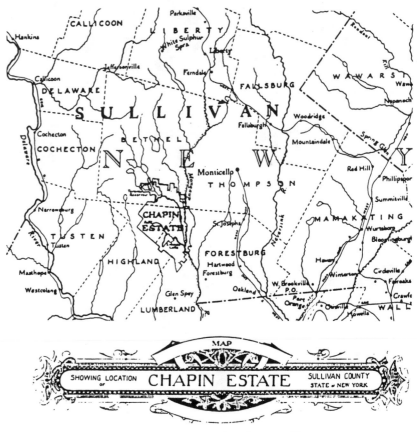

The 18,000-acre Chapin estate in southwestern Sullivan County. The Conservation Commission built a fire tower on the estate's Chapin Hill in 1924.

Orange Rockland Utilities, Inc.

"I was sad to see the tower taken down," comments Joe Keegan, the forestry supervisor for the utility company. "I used to enjoy visiting the observer and eating my lunch up in the tower. It was a landmark that I wish had been saved."

Lore

CLAIRE SHIELLS'S HUSBAND, HARRY, worked at the tower from 1935 to 1939. She says, "Harry, knew the land like the back of his hand. He grew up on the Chapin Estate where his dad was the gamekeeper. He worked to stop the poachers."

Above: **Chapin Park Tower.** Carol O'Neill

Facing page, clockwise from upper left:

Bernard "Bun" O'Neill was the Chapin Hill observer from 1939 to 1947 and forest ranger from 1948 to 1953. Carol O'Neill and Elsie O'Neill Bisland

Observer Marge O'Neill (1960-66) and her husband, Forest Ranger Charlie O'Neill (1954-81) worked together in fire detection and suppression in Sullivan County. Charlie also served as an observer at Graham Fire Tower (1953-54). Marge O'Neill

Francis Weber was the observer on Chapin Hill for three years. He was transferred to Graham Fire Tower and was known as a hard worker. Mildred Weber

Charlie Houghtaling of Port Jervis was the observer at Chapin Hill (1957-59) and Graham (1967?-69) fire towers. Marty Podskoch

A new cabin was constructed by the state in 1942.
Carol O'Neill

* * *

Elsie O'Neill Bisland remembers her wedding day. "It was May 16, 1939, and my husband-to-be, Bernie 'Bun' O'Neill, was busy working at his new job. He was the fire tower observer at Chapin Hill, and he said there were fires all over the surrounding area. Bun felt that he was desperately needed at the tower to communicate with the fire fighters. Meanwhile, I was at home anxiously awaiting him. Would he be home on time for the evening wedding? I was getting more nervous as the hour of the wedding drew near. I hadn't heard from him because I didn't have a phone. Then I saw him drive up, and we made it to the Methodist Church in Sparrowbush just in the nick of time."

* * *

Ranger Charlie O'Neill remembers: "Trains coming down the mountains on the Graham line into Port Jervis would throw off red-hot pieces of brake shoes and sparks from the stacks. The westbound train from Port Jervis to Calicoon traveling along the Delaware River also caused fires."

* * *

Ranger O'Neill's wife, Marge, worked as observer at Chapin Hill from 1960 to 1966. After a quiet day, she was about to leave and pick up her young boys who were at her friend Kathy Bisland's house. Turning her eyes from the panorama of sky and forest to her little car far below, she saw something in the mown grass that caused her heart to skip a beat.

Marge focused on three large rattlesnakes sunning themselves in the space around her car. "It was only a few hundred feet," she recalls, "but I did not want to chance it. I was too far from help if I was bitten, so I called Charlie. He calmed me down and said he would be right over. I continued to look for smoke but the snakes were my real concern. By the time Charlie arrived, the snakes had disappeared into the nearby woods, and I was relieved."

This was not the only close encounter Marge had with wild animals. "Sometimes during the summers, my boys came to work with me," recalls O'Neill. "One time when the two youngest, Gary and Lash, were with me, I parked the car by the picnic table. We headed to the steps of the tower. To our left was a commotion made by a mother bear and two very little cubs. Instead

of going in the woods, she was heading in our direction. We were close to the steps and ran up as fast as we could. The bears ran between us and the car into the woods. The boys thought that was great! I did not!

"I drove a tiny Fiat convertible to the tower. Believe me, it *was* tiny. One day there was a very large rattlesnake crossing my little dirt road. He looked enormous from that little car. I was afraid to run over him so I waited until he got out of the road and into the woods.

"Another day, I met a bear coming toward me while I was on my way home. He looked as large as my little car, and I didn't think he was going to stop coming. I stopped and kept blowing my horn. Finally, he shook his head a few times, and nonchalantly walked into the woods. A man in a pickup coming in the opposite direction saw this, too. He couldn't believe it either. He said, 'Maybe we shouldn't say anything about it because nobody will believe us.'"

O'Neill describes the cabin near the fire tower as quite primitive: "It had three small rooms, no electricity, and no water. I had to carry water in. There was very little furniture because most of the observers, like me, didn't stay overnight."

"There was a two-seater outhouse," recalls Marge. "I tried not to use it very often because of my fear of snakes, especially rattlers, which the area was well noted for. There were some active rattlesnake dens on the O&R [Orange & Rockland Utilities] property and DEC employee Joe Roberty used to hunt them."

Marge O'Neill remembers problems resulting from the weather. "One afternoon I was sitting in the tower and there was a light rain. Then it turned really cold and the rain turned to freezing ice. I didn't get down soon enough. All the metal and wood were covered with ice. . .it was just too slippery. I took off my sneakers and went down in my socks. My hands and feet felt frozen after my very slow long trip down all those steps. I don't remember how many steps there were, but there sure were a lot of them.

"Another time I was up in the tower on a foggy morning. I couldn't see the ground or the cabin, but I did smell smoke. I alerted my ranger, who was in the area with some fire wardens. They couldn't find anything. Finally, when the sun came out, the haze burned off and there was the fire heading right at my tower! Within minutes forest rangers together with fire wardens and their crews began to battle the blaze. My tower was the base of the operation. I had more company that day than I had had in the previous seven years."

* * *

Retired observer Charlie Houghtaling, now living in Port Jervis, had an interesting experience driving from the tower. Charlie noticed the body of a doe and her fawn lying along the road. They had probably been hit by a vehicle. As he drove slowly by the bodies he heard bleating from the woods. He stopped to investigate and found another fawn alive, obviously the twin. Charlie brought the orphaned fawn home and he and his wife, Lillian, raised it.

Lillian says, "Someone told us to feed it lime water and milk. We kept it in our house. It was funny when it would look at itself in a mirror. Then we made a pen for it outside. We kept it for a year or more and then Charlie let it go free near his hunting camp at Big Pond Road." The deer lived for many years in the surrounding woods. "She would come near our camp and the kids hand-fed her. She was so friendly the kids would ride on her back. Every year she had a set of twins. She would keep them behind a rock wall while she came to us for food."

H. Vincent Masten was the observer from 1925 to 1927. After the war, he worked again at Chapin Hill from 1948 to 1952. One of his sons was born in the observer's cabin in 1925. John Masten

Charlie continues, "We found her dead one day even though she had a ribbon that we put on her neck to protect her during hunting season. It probably was a drive-by hunter who shot her."

* * *

Albert Woolsey Jr. remembers his father working at the tower in 1967: "My father had Lou Gehrig's disease and had trouble climbing the stairs. Once he got up, he stayed there. He said he saw every kind of animal except a mountain lion. He would throw his lunch out to the visiting deer. He even had names for them."

* * *

Because Chapin Hill tower was on private property, it had few visitors. The observers' families, however, liked to visit the tower. John and Bernice Masten of Wurtsboro visited John's father, Vincent. "Near the cabin there was a picnic table and a stone fireplace," says John. "We would have picnics on the weekend."

Bernice adds, "My father-in-law was a great man. I enjoyed sitting up in the tower and listening to him tell stories. He loved the outdoors and the wild animals that passed through the area near the cabin and tower."

Of the last observer at Chapin Hill, Francis Weber of Glen Spey (1968-70), DEC Captain Ray Wood says, "He was always working. He maintained the road whenever there was a washout. It was as smooth as a paved road."

Observers

Charles Ollech (1924), Harold Vincent Masten (1925-27), Howard Van Tyle (1928-31), William Driscoll (1932-33), Harry Shiells (1935-39), Bernard O'Neill (1939-47), H. Vincent Masten (1948-52), Gaylord Law or Lowe (1953-54?), Charles Houghtaling (1957-59), Marge O'Neill (1960-66), Albert Woolsey (1967), Francis Weber (1968-70).

Rangers

Ralph Phillips (1925-59) and Charles R. O'Neill (1960-81).

11. Gallis Hill, 1927

History

IN 1927, the Conservation Department erected a tower and observer's cabin on Gallis Hill (780 feet), a few miles west of Kingston near Route 28. The tower provided additional protection for the eastern Catskills; however, it was located outside the Forest Preserve. John E. Haynes, the first observer, did not report any fires in 1927 but did note 100 visitors who registered at the tower. The following year, observer Haynes reported 14 fires and and recorded 445 visitors; in 1929, 79 fires and 539 visitors.[78]

During the 1930s, observer George Edson reported many fires: 56 in 1935, 65 in 1938 and 28 in 1939. Then in the 1940s, the number of reported fires decreased to 25 in 1944 and zero 1945.[79]

In 1950, the Conservation Department moved the tower eight miles north of Woodstock to Overlook Mountain, which had a better view of the eastern Catskills. The Gallis Hill Fire Tower site is privately owned and not accessible to the public.

Lore

LOUISE H. FLOOD, a Kingston resident, remembers when her grandfather, John Haynes, was a fire observer on Gallis Hill from 1927 to 1929. "My grandfather kept a log of the temperature and wind conditions," she says. "In his diary he noted the visibility for the day, the atmospheric conditions and the locations of the fires spotted. He also included the times he was granted a day by his superior to have treatments for the carcinoma on his foot and to attend a relative's funeral."

John Haynes stayed at the cabin with his wife, who walked down each morning to help her daughter keep a boardinghouse on Route 28. Mrs. Haynes baked pies, picked berries and ironed. Each night she trekked up to the cabin with an Adirondack pack on her back,

John E. Haynes, observer on Gallis Hill from 1927 to 1929, in front of the observer's cabin.

Louise Flood.

carrying food for her husband while keeping a wary eye for copperheads and rattlesnakes along the trail.

Because the road was usually in poor condition, Louise's grandparents used a horse-drawn wagon to haul their furniture and valuables to the cabin in the spring and to return them in the fall. After two years, John had to give up his job because of his health.

George Edson, the second observer, lived in the observer's cabin with his family. During the school year, Edson walked his son down the mountain to Route 28. William O'Kelly, a teacher who was Haynes' son-in-law, picked up the boy and drove him to their one-room schoolhouse. Later, the road was improved and Edson kept a car at the cabin.

Flood remembers, "Visitors to the tower parked in our yard on Route 28. They walked the footpath that my grandmother used to get to the tower. The hikers carried sticks to beat off poisonous snakes living in the hilltop scrub oak and huckleberry bushes."

Louise Flood often walked the trail with her aunt. She says, "I enjoyed seeing and smelling the beautiful flowering trees. There were arbutus, dogwood and shadblow. On the ground I saw dogtooth violets, adder's tongue, lady slippers, jack-in-the-pulpit, mayflowers, and fuzzy stemmed hepatica.

"I had a great imagination. I pictured the fire tower as Colossus astride the mountain. It wasn't difficult to envision Aeolus puffing his cheeks when the enclosure shuddered and swayed on its legs.

"For nearly 100 years these metal Titans have existed in our Catskills. Let's hope they will not remain on the endangered species list," concludes Louise Flood.

Observers

John E. Haynes (1927-29), George Edson (1930-44), Jacob Schilling (1945), Phillip Scully (1946-47), Raymond Winne (1949), Joseph Gilbert (1950).

Rangers

David Hillson (1919-45), Aaron Van De Bogart (1942, 1945-71).

Front and back of the cards observers gave to hikers.

12. Pocatello, 1930

History

ON DECEMBER 11, 1929, the Orange County Board of Supervisors appropriated $1,000 toward the construction of a fire tower to protect the eastern and southern slopes of the Shawangunk Mountains. Private funds were used, also. Pocatello Mountain (830 feet) near Middletown was selected as the site for the tower and observer's cabin.

In 1930, Conservation Department workers completed construction and installed a telephone line. Three years later, an electric line was run to the tower to power a radio that allowed Pocatello observers to talk with state pilots as they patrolled the area.

Ranger Earl Brewer, an amateur radio man, worked with observer John Behrens to set up a Conservation Department radio station at Pocatello Fire Tower. During 1938, the station, WIXBE, was on the air for 510 hours and 35 minutes.

"In 1948, the state moved the Pocatello Fire Tower to Graham on the Shawangunk Mountains," remembers Fire Warden Dave Brinckerhoff of Middletown. "This gave the observer a better view of Orange County because it was 1,310 feet high compared to Pocatello Mountain, which was only 830 feet."

* * *

I contacted Mike Myers, the outdoor sports writer for *The Middletown Record*, to help me find the site of the Pocatello Fire Tower. He was a perfect guide because he had grown up in the area. We met one Saturday morning at the Pocatello Fire House in Middletown. Mike took me about a mile up the road and turned onto a narrow road to Lake Pocatello. After parking our cars at the end, we climbed a narrow moss-covered road to the summit. There an old lime-colored cabin sat on a narrow ridge. The windows and door were knocked out, and there were two charred holes on the porch floor. The rest of the cabin was

The Pocatello Fire Tower was built on Pocatello Mountain in 1930.
Daniel Smiley Research Center

intact. Four concrete piers stood in front of the cabin, the remnants of the 60-foot steel tower.

The Pocatello Fire Tower was taken down in 1949 and moved to Graham near Otisville.

Lore

JOHN BEHRENS, who manned the Pocatello tower in 1944 and 1945, was a pioneer in the development of

74

radio communications for the Conservation Department. Behrens's wife, Dot, still lives in the small cottage at Wanaksink Lake where John developed the portable radio. She says, "In 1934, John volunteered to be a fire warden and worked with District Ranger Leon Fursch. He [John] was fascinated with radios. John developed a portable radio the state used to control a fire during the spring of 1935. He also developed the first successful portable radio-airplane communication system used on a forest fire."

* * *

Bear Mountain Forest Ranger Tim Sullivan remembers: "I used to work with John in the garage behind his cottage on Wanaksink Lake. It was a radio repair junk shop. We traveled all over the state installing and repairing the state's radio equipment."

John was known as a practical joker. "I'll never forget the time I was up in the Jackie Jones Fire Tower near Bear Mountain," Sullivan continues. "John called me up on the radio and said, 'I'm having trouble hearing you. Take off the back of your radio and put your screwdriver next to the button. Now turn up the volume.' Wow!! I got the shock of my life. I jumped up into the air so high I almost touched the roof. This was followed by quite a few curses."

Behrens also played a practical joke on Graham tower observer Steve Canfield. "I was just a young guy, and John sent me on an errand in the state truck. I was driving a Dodge Power Wagon down this country road, and I heard some movement under my seat. Then out came a snapping turtle by my feet. As I tried to fight it off, I went off the road and crashed through a farmer's fence. I jumped out of the truck and dragged the snapper out with a council rake. Boy, that John really knew how to get to you."

* * *

The tower was supervised by the local forest ranger, Earl Brewer, who worked at the Pocatello and Graham towers for more than 30 years. "He was a heavy-set gentleman," recalls Dave Brinckerhoff. "He did a lot of fire fighting with my father, Gilbert, who was a fire warden. Earl was instrumental in building up the Fire Warden Association. The wardens became pretty powerful. If there was a fire and Earl needed

men, he could stop a car and demand that you help with a fire. If you refused, you could be prosecuted. Earl would go right into the school and take some high school boys to fight the fires. Then the principal got upset, and he had to stop."

Observers

Leon Custer (1931-42), John Behrens (1944-45), W. G. Smith (1946-48).

Ranger

Earl Brewer (1931-61)

John F. Behrens. Dot Behrens

75

13. Mount Utsayantha, 1934

History

AFTER PURCHASING 20 ACRES at the top of 3,214-foot Mount Utsayantha near Stamford in western Delaware County, Colonel Rulif W. Rulifson built the first of several towers. On July 4, 1882, he opened it to the public. The wooden pyramidal structure was four stories high and boasted a glass-enclosed room and an open observation deck that afforded tourists a commanding view of forests and mountains. It was a refreshing sight after the long train trip from New York City.

Four times, in 1892, 1895, 1901 and 1916, strong winds blew down the Rulifson tower, and each time it was rebuilt, with later reconstructions relying on steel cables to anchor the structure. Despite threats from high winds, the tower was joined on the mountain by a 20-by-30-foot frame "hotel," which cost $1000 to build. According to Stamford historian Anne Willis, "Tourists rode wagons to the top where they were served a nice chicken dinner. When they got up in the morning, it was a thrill to watch the sunrise."

A Georgia man named M. McDevitt nearly completed construction of a three-story hotel on land he

Above: **An early wooden observation tower on Mount Utsayantha.** Mark Haughwout Collection
Facing page: **The fire tower and observer's cabin in 1997.** Marty Podskoch

The wooden observatory, once used by Native Americans who sold souvenirs, still stands but in poor repair.
Cordy Rich Collection

purchased near the summit, but it burned down in 1881 before it opened. The remains of its foundation are still visible.

The next owner of the mountain was Dr. S. E. Churchill. In 1910, he installed an acetylene searchlight on top of the mountain that could be seen for 20 miles. Older residents say the light served as a beacon for early pilots. When Churchill died, he willed the top of Mount Utsayantha to the Village of Stamford.

In 1934, Civilian Conservation Corps (CCC) workers built a 68-foot fire tower on Mount Utsayantha at a cost of $260. During its first year of operation in 1935, observer Alton Henderson reported 13 fires, and 450 people visited the tower. In 1937, four fires were spotted and 1,581 visitors were recorded. Visitation increased over the years, and in 1957, 3,100 signed the register. Observer James E. Davies reported five fires that year.

The tower was officially closed by the DEC in 1989. It is still standing but is not maintained by the state. Vandals have destroyed about half of the cabin.

Lore

MOUNT UTSAYANTHA got its name from the legend of a local Indian maiden, Utsayantha. She was said to have borne a child whose father was white, something that made Utsayantha's father, the chief, so furious he buried his tomahawk in the white man's skull and rowed with the baby to the center of a lake and drowned it. Utsayantha followed her father to the lake and drowned herself, too. The legend says the chief

then carried her body up the mountain, where he buried her. This legend has attracted many visitors to the mountain.

In 1960, Grey Wolf, a Native American, and his family lived in the white observatory building at the summit and sold souvenirs. More than 7,500 tourists from 13 counties and 30 states visited his "Indian village." He fashioned the totem pole that is now in the Stamford Village Park.

* * *

While working for the DEC in the 1970s, observer Al Jordan of Franklin remembers painting the tower: "We opened the windows and put a board out. One guy sat on the board in the cab and another stood outside on the extended board. The state required us to wear a rope harness in case we fell. Well, I decided to climb on the roof and paint it without a rope," says Jordan. "Then I noticed a state car coming up the road, and I knew I was in trouble. I quickly got off the roof. The official came up to the cab and said to me, 'I saw that you didn't have a safety rope on.' I told him that if I had a rope and fell off the 68-foot tower, I'd probably bang my head on the steel and be a vegetable the rest of my life. 'This way, if I fall, I'll die instantly.' He looked at me a while and said, 'You're probably right.' He didn't write me up."

* * *

The Southern New York Hang Glider Pilots Association held frequent competitions at Utsayantha in the 1980s with some hang gliders flying as far east as Kingston and as far west as Whitney Point. On at least one occasion, observer Clifton Oakley was certain the hang glider taking off from a ramp below his tower was headed for disaster: "I thought for sure that he was going down in the trees. But he kept circling around like a buzzard. They get in those thermals and go a long way. Then he was soaring above me and the tower." The club still holds an annual meet on Mount Utsayantha on Memorial Day weekend.

Another time, Oakley saw a few boys who had played on the summit before starting back down a trail. "Soon after," he says, "I saw a fire observation plane coming toward the tower. 'Hey Cliff,' the pilot radioed, 'do you know you've got a fire on your mountain?'"

"I didn't, so I looked down the trail that the boys had taken a little while before, and to my surprise, I saw smoke. I couldn't believe that some boys did that, and a plane saw the fire before me. That was a little embarrassing."

Oakley and Grace were not without amenities. They had electricity and, says Oakley, "We were the only ones in the area who could get up to 41 channels on the TV."

From the top of the tower, Oakley could see 50 miles. But even the remarkable view could prove tedious. "To kill time in the tower I would read magazines," he says. His shifts lasted five days at a time, including weekends, when the greatest number of fires occurred.

* * *

Oakley's son, Don, manned the tower in 1979 and 1980. He says, "I loved working at the tower, but one day I had a scary thing happen to me: I was sitting in the tower, and it was really foggy. I heard a motor that sounded like a helicopter, and it was getting closer and closer. Then about 40 yards from me, I saw a helicopter coming right at me and the tower. The pilot was fast on the stick, and he just veered off to the side of the tower. That was the scariest thing that happened to me."

Observers

Alton Henderson (1936-41), James E. Davies (1942-62), Merton Van Deusen (1963-71), Thomas Brown (1972), Larry D. Germond, Perry M. Miller Jr. (1973), Kenneth Greek (1974-75), Allan Jordan (1976-78), Donald Oakley (1979-80), Judy Merwin (1981), Clifton Oakley (1982-89).

Rangers

David T. Williams (1937-44), Noel Gonyo (1948-68), Peter Rossi (1968-89).

Directions

Turn south on Mountain Road at the east edge of Stamford on Route 23. Near the top, turn left onto the dirt road. You can park there and walk the one mile to the summit. As you travel the dirt road, you will see a granite grave marker, the alleged burial spot of the Indian maiden Utsayantha.

Observer Clifton Oakley of Grand Gorge and his wife, Grace, lived at the Mount Utsayantha Fire Tower during the 1980s.

Marty Podskoch

79

14. Gilbert Lake, 1934

History

IN 1934, young men at the CCC Camp at Gilbert Lake State Park built an 80-foot fire tower on a 1,790-foot hill. They staffed the tower, and Army Reserve officers supervised the camp until it closed in October 1941. The Conservation Department did not staff the tower during this period. In 1948, the state moved the tower to Leonard Hill in Schoharie County.

Lore

FINDING NO WORK in Oneonta during the Depression, many young men joined the CCC camp at Gilbert Lake. "I started at the CCC camp in April of 1934, but I never manned the tower," says Willie Ronovech. "I took a lot of pictures of the camp, and one of them is of the fire tower. After working all day, I'd walk up the hill in the evening. I wasn't scared to climb the tower. When I got to the top, there was quite a view from the cab. Some of our jobs at the camp were planting trees and fighting fires. Once we helped the people of Delhi during a flood."

August "Augie" Gardella began working as an observer on July 1, 1934. He says, "One guy worked 12 hours, and the next day I worked for 12 hours. We started at 8:00 in the morning and worked till 8:00 at night. I did this for three months, but I never spotted a fire. The cab was equipped with a phone to call the main office if there was a fire. The job was enjoyable, and I wished I had it the following year."

Augie read a lot of books when he wasn't talking to the children and parents who were visiting the park. "They asked me questions and loved the view."

On weekends, young men from the CCC went to dances in Oneonta. Two camp trucks carried them to town to find entertainment. Augie remembers going to Dreamland Gardens: "When we got to the bar, we bought one bottle of beer for a quarter and nursed it the whole night. We were so happy to go dancing and

Members of the CCC Camp at Gilbert Lake State Park, Laurens, New York, in 1935. They built the 80-foot fire tower that was moved to Leonard Hill, Schoharie County in 1948. "Augie" Gardella is the 11th person from the right in the third row. Willie Ronoveck is the fourth person from the right in the first row. Augie Gardella

meet some pretty girls. Many times we missed the truck and had to hitchhike back to Laurens. Then, at about 1:30 A.M., we walked three miles up to the camp. We had pleasant memories of dancing with the pretty girls, but we were so tired, I think we were sleep-walking."

The young men lived in barracks. "Forty guys lived in one building. During the winter there were two coal stoves that we stoked to keep warm," says Oneontan Carl Delberta. "It was a good life because there weren't many jobs for people during the Depression."

* * *

Irving Reed, a retired Delhi teacher, grew up in the farming community of Columbus Quarter near South Edmeston. "We had a Columbus Quarter Community Club that met once a month at various homes," recalls Reed. "Each summer one meeting was held at Gilbert Lake State Park. The younger crowd walked up the path to the fire tower and rushed to climb the 80-foot tower. At the top of the stairs, we raised the trap door and enjoyed the spectacular views. We looked forward to the visit every year."

* * *

Today, the site of the fire tower holds a baseball field near the Hilltop camping area. Park Manager Ed Winslow took Augie Gardella and me to see if we could find footings or any other trace of the old tower. We found none but concluded that it had been either near the woods or near home plate.

Directions

A CCC museum, open to the public, is located by the Gilbert Lake State Park swimming area and bathhouse. Park Manager Ed Winslow says, "Les Bush came up with the idea for the museum, and Richard Ranieri organized the materials and displays. There are many pictures showing the activities of the CCC and tools that they used."

From Oneonta take Interstate 88 west to Route 205 (Exit 13). Follow 205 to Laurens and take County Route 12 west to the park entrance.

Gilbert Lake State Park Fire Tower built by the CCC camp and manned from 1934 to 1941.
William Ronovech

15. Rock Rift, 1934

History

IN 1934, Civilian Conservation Corps boys built a 68-foot steel tower on Rock Rift Mountain (2,382 feet) in the Town of Tompkins, Delaware County, ten miles south of Walton near today's Cannonsville Reservoir. "They also built the cabin and the road to the tower and set up the spring," says Ogden Foote, a Walton resident.

"The fire tower site was originally owned by Moses Edwards," says Edward Stanton, Manager of the Office of Claims for the New York City Bureau of Water Supply (NYCBWS) in Downsville. "On June 27, 1957, the city bought land parcel #3580 from Moses' son, Leslie I. Edwards. It was a long narrow piece of land that went to the top of the mountain where the state fire tower is located."

Today New York City still owns the land surrounding the tower, but the structure itself is owned by the DEC. "The only people who have access to the tower are the DEC," says Jack Kane of the NYCBWS in Downsville. "It is unlikely that the city will open the land for hiking because of the liability problem."

Linda Trask was the last observer at the tower in 1988. To get to her post, she used a dirt road on land owned by George Huntington. The road started on Route 10 near the Apex Bridge and climbed the mountain.

Tim Robinson of Walton says, "Linda was very devoted to her job, and she was quite upset when they closed the tower." The tower and cabin were not maintained by the DEC and deteriorated. In the winter of 1998, vandals burned the cabin, but the tower still stands.

Lore

FORMER OBSERVER REX SCOFIELD says, "I grew up in the shadow of the tower and it greatly affected my life. My father, Leslie, had a stone quarry about 100 yards below the Rock Rift Fire Tower. During the summer, my whole family lived in a one-room cabin near the quarry. We kept goats for milk, and we had a vegetable garden. We were always going to the tower and visiting the fire observer. I used to spend a lot of time with the old observers."

The first observer at the tower was James Van de Mark, known locally as Jimmy Brown. "In the winter, Jimmy would work at my father's quarry," says Scofield.

* * *

John W. Northrop was the second fire observer. He started in 1943 and worked for about five years. Neal Northrup, who was not related to John, remembers meeting the observer when Northrup worked at the Scofield quarry: "I was about 12 or 14, and John would visit us in the quarry. John was a kind of hillbilly, mountaineer person, but he had a lot of knowledge. He drove to the tower in a 1933 Chevrolet with a rumble seat."

"John was an old man who lived with his wife in the cabin," remembers Scofield. "She would sit on the porch and sew buttons on a bed sheet, and no two buttons were alike. Sometimes Northrop would go into Walton, and if he saw that you had an unusual button, he would rip it right off your coat or shirt. His wife had hundreds of sheets with buttons sewn on, but she never sold any."

Facing page, clockwise from top left:

Rock Rift Fire Tower cabin in spring 1997. It was vandalized more that year and burned down. Marty Podskoch

The tower in 1997. It is located on reservoir land and is not accessible to the public. Marty Podskoch

Observer Linda Trask (1966-88) shows children how she uses the alidade on the circular table map to pinpoint a fire. Linda Trask

Observer Jimmy Brown (1936-41) working at a rock quarry near the Rock Rift Fire Tower.
Rex Scofield

* * *

"In 1948, Marzell Hubbell became the third observer. Everyone called him 'Bogue Dumont.' He was raised by the DuMont family and he limped pretty bad," says Scofield. "Bogue was a great storyteller. He would sit in his chair with a bear hide on it. People would usually visit on Sundays and have picnics. Everyone would gather on the porch, and he would tell fantastic stories."

Scofield remembers when he was young and a group of boys were listening intently to a bear story:

"Bogue would say how he and I shot the bear. The boys were so amazed that I helped shoot a bear. I felt so proud."

The observers enjoyed the visitors because they often brought sumptuous picnics and always invited the observers to share in the feast. "Sometimes we had five or ten cars come up on a Sunday afternoon for a family picnic," says Scofield who staffed the tower in 1956. "I was newly married to my wife, Jean, and I loved being in the woods. I had to quit the next year because I was just starting a family, and the pay was quite low."

Scofield remembers one foggy morning when he was reading in the tower. "All of a sudden I heard this plane buzzing past the tower, and I could see the two people in the cockpit. The wing just missed the cab."

* * *

Retired Walton fire fighter, Jim Olmstead, remembers getting a fire call for Fishs Brook. "Scofield was in the tower, and he saw this huge cloud of smoke coming up the cliff. It was a big fire. It started at a logger's camp and went straight up the cliff. The fire was probably started by loggers working for Sam Sukoff. He was notorious for bringing men from the Bowery and leaving them in the woods. There was another time when a cabin caught on fire and a man died inside."

* * *

During the 1970s, a forest ranger brought some of his daughter's Girl Scout Troop up the wooden stairs of the tower. They came to learn how the observer spotted forest fires. They finally reached the last landing, and the wooden trap door opened. Linda Trask beckoned to the girls, who were now 68 feet in the air, and they entered the cab.

Trask showed the girls how she pinpointed fires. The girls were interested in all the details, but one girl tapped Linda on the shoulder: "Excuse me, Miss Trask, but isn't that smoke coming from those mountains down there?" "That was pretty embarrassing, that little girl spotting a fire before me," remembers Trask.

* * *

Hundreds of local residents visited the tower each year. They went south on Route 10 to Bob's Brook Road and then turned left on Walton Mountain Road and again on Tower Road. Today, this road is closed. Real estate developer Tim Robinson explains, "The road was closed because part of it was washed out." Today the tower is inaccessible from Tower Road because hikers cannot walk through posted New York City and private land.

"I'd love to see the fire towers restored because they're an historical part of the region, just like the covered bridges that I fought to save," says Perry Shelton, retired Tompkins town supervisor. "They tell the history of the county, the way we lived." Shelton suggests obtaining permission from land owners and the city to open a trail to the tower. "Then even old people like me could have a short, level walk to the tower."

Observers

James Van de Mark "Jimmy Brown" (1936-41), J. W. Northrop Sr. (1942-47), Bruce Webster (1948), Marzell Hubbell (1948-54), Ross Schlafer (1955), Rexford Scofield (1956), Hobart "Jubie" Brown (1956-65), Linda Trask (1966-1988).

Rangers

Leon Johnson (1932-1960), Walt Teuber (1961-88), Ed Hale (1968-?).

Rex Scofield enjoyed visiting the observers and listening to their stories. He became the observer himself in 1956.
Rex Scofield

16. Hooker Hill, 1934

History

HOOKER HILL is located four miles northeast of Schenevus in the Town of Maryland in Otsego County. The mountain was named after Robert Hooker, who purchased it on April 5, 1848, from William Nellis.

"In the early 1900s, Louis Chermack, my grandfather, bought the hill," recalls Florence Chermack Dulkis. "He was in ill health in New York City and retired to the country. He raised a small herd of cows." In 1934, Chermack's wife, Gisella, gave New York State the right to construct, operate and maintain a fire tower on their property.

Conservation Department officials chose Hooker Hill because it was central to a state forest. Tower observers worked in tandem with those at Mount Utsayantha Fire Tower in Stamford, using triangulation to pinpoint a fire to within 1/8 of a mile.

The state had acquired the tower from the U. S. Forest Service in 1933, and it was shipped by rail to Oneonta in 1934. CCC workers from Camp #93-S at Breakabeen constructed the foundation, and the Conservation Department installed a telephone line connecting the tower with the Town of Maryland operator in Schenevus. The tower opened on April 1, 1936; William J. Gill of Maryland was the first observer.

Hooker Hill's observer spotted many fires started by Delaware & Hudson Railroad trains as they traveled beside Route 7. Volunteer fireman Donald Trask of Schenevus remembers fighting fires started from sparks spewing from the trains' smokestacks: "The sparks landed on the dry grass and brush along the tracks. Sparks also came from the 'boxen,' a place near the axle

Louis Chermack's barn and house on Hooker Mountain about 1938. The fire tower is visible on the ridge.
Florence Chermack Dulkis

86

where the trainmen put oil. If they didn't oil the axle, sparks would develop and fly out and start a fire."

In 1970, after 35 years of service, the DEC closed Hooker Hill Fire Tower. Forest rangers removed the lower stairs in 1971 because they were concerned that someone might be injured.

In 1975, the state put the fire tower up for bids. Alan Jordan purchased it for $490. He says, "I always wanted a tower on the mountain on my farm in Franklin. I had fun taking it down. It was like playing with an Erector set. It took me three days to take down. A boy loaded it on my truck while I lowered him the pieces. I dug the holes for the footings eight feet deep.

"Because it was going to be very expensive, I put the project off and I never got the tower up. It is still in a pile. I sure would like to put it up sometime."

In 1979, the State Police received permission from the land owners to build a radio transmitter on the old fire tower site. Today the site is owned by Richard J. Long of the Town of Maryland and is not accessible to the public.

Lore

ROBERT HOOKER of Long Lake in the Adirondacks says, "My great-great-grandfather, Robert Hooker, owned the mountain and my family farmed the land for many years. My family enjoyed going to the Hooker tower when I was young."

* * *

During the spring and fall of the late 1950s, William Sutton manned the tower. As he looked out toward the northwestern part of the Catskill Mountains, he heard voices from people climbing the 80-foot steel tower. He opened the floor hatchway of his cab and his teenage son, Donald, poked his head in. Don's friend, Ernie Mickle, followed him into the small, seven-foot wide cab.

"What are you two guys doing up here? Why aren't you in school?" Sutton asked.

The boys' excuse was plausible so when they asked Sutton if he would play cards with them--they knew he loved to play pitch-- he agreed.

"OK, but you boys have to go back to school so you don't get me in trouble," replied Sutton.

After a few hands of cards, the players heard heavy footsteps. Then the hatch lifted and Vince Ciliberti climbed into the crowded room. A big, strong man, Vince was the gym teacher and truant officer at Schenevus High School.

"What are you guys doing up here? You're supposed to be in school! Now let's go!" commanded the truant officer.

Observer William Sutton Sr. (1955-59) enjoyed frequent visits from his family.
Marge Sutton Vaughn.

"Well, that ended our playing hooky, and Dad swore to Vince that he didn't know that we were cutting school," remembers Donald.

Sutton's daughter, Marge Vaughn of Wells Bridge, recalls, "Almost every day I rode my bike to see my Dad at the tower. It was about a five-mile bike ride, and it was uphill. We were inseparable. I loved to watch him work and calculate the location of a fire."

* * *

As a teenager, Stanley Barnes often hiked to the tower from his home in Schenevus. He recalls, "On a Saturday afternoon my friends and I hiked from the village. It was something to do. We went up Sperry Hollow to North Road and then through state land to the fire tower. It took about two hours to get there. Sometimes the observer wasn't there because the state kept a person in the tower only during the spring and fall, when there was a threat of fire. We climbed the tower and just opened the hatch door. You could see all the way to Stamford and see the Mount Utsayantha Fire Tower. We even saw the fire tower at Gilbert Lake State Park. The view was spectacular."

Barnes, a retired fire chief of Schenevus says, "If the observer saw a fire, he called the local telephone operator in Schenevus. The operator called Wick's Restaurant, and the waitress blew the fire siren. Today communication has really improved. More people live in the area, and if they spot a fire, they have cell phones and CBs to call for help."

* * *

One visitor to the tower was a big surprise: "My dad, Don Beaudin, owned the Westville Airport. He taught me to fly when I was young," recalls Gail Beaudin Pierce. "I flew up the side of Hooker Hill and then zoomed right toward the tower. I buzzed the tower and scared the tower observer so bad that he jumped back in fright. He landed right on the floor. You should have seen the terror in his eyes."

* * *

Janice Tubbs, daughter of observer Ralph Tubbs, says, "My Dad loved his job. When he wasn't in the tower, he helped Ranger Don Secord on state park projects."

Sometimes rangers had difficulties getting fire observers. Ranger Secord remembers hiring one man, Cappy Kenyon. "I showed him how to spot fires and notify me. Well, the next day I called him on the radio, but there was no answer. So, I drove up to see if he was there. When I got to the tower, there was Cappy sitting in his truck. I said, 'Why didn't you answer the radio?' He replied, 'Sorry Don, but I was afraid of the radio.' That was one guy who didn't even last one day."

The Hooker Fire Tower in 1966.
Robert Parmerter

Observers

William Gill (1936-42), Elmer D. Cady (1943-54), William Sutton Sr. (1955-59), Edward F. Dubben (1960-62), Robert A. Nelson (1962-65), Ralph C. Tubbs (1966-70), Julian Cole (fall of 1970).

Rangers

John W. Chase (1931-1950), Glenmore Carrington (1951-60), Bill Sussdorf (1960-65), Don "Lou" Secord (1964-1975).

17. Page Pond, 1936

History

IN 1935, the Conservation Department acquired an easement to build a fire tower on the 120-acre Mike Hromada farm at the top of Page Pond Hill (2,040 feet).

The state received help in constructing the 80-foot steel tower from CCC Camp P-76, which was established on November 11, 1933, along old Route 17 between McClure and Deposit in Delaware County. CCC workers transported the tower materials via Page Pond Road, which ran through Amahami, a Girl Scout camp on Page Pond since 1929.

During the tower's second year of operation, 1937, the observer reported 12 fires; 29 visitors signed the register. In 1960, 33 fires were spotted and 346 people visited the tower. The state operated the fire tower, and maintained the cabin and telephone line, until the fire tower closed in 1988.

Ed Engelman, a 20-year camp ranger at Amahami Girl Scout camp, stated, "In 1960, the Girl Scouts purchased the Mike Hromada farm, where the fire tower was. From the tower you could see four large pieces of state forest. When the Girl Scouts heard that the state was trying to dispose of the tower in the early 1990s, they talked to the state about acquiring the tower and cabin."

DEC records in Albany show that no one wanted to buy the tower. It would have cost the state about $15,000 to remove it, so the state gave the tower, cabin and outbuildings to the Girl Scouts Indian Hills Council, Inc. in December 1992.

Lore

USUALLY Harry Halpin watched for fires by day from the Page Pond Fire Tower. But one cold fall evening in 1949, Harry was atop the fire tower searching for something else when he heard a shout echoing through the valley below.

"Hey, I got one! Wait until I turn on the light!"

As a beam of light pierced the darkness, a loud bang reverberated through the forest. It was not a gun shot, however, but the sharp clanging of the trap door in the fire tower cab.

C.C.C. CO. NO. 211, CAMP NO. P-76, DEPOSIT, N. Y., MAY, 1935, CAPT. *Werner C. Strecker* ENGR-RES. COM'D'G

Workers from CCC Camp P-76 built the Page Pond Fire Tower in 1934.
Amahami Girl Scout Camp

"My husband, Harry, was a very good sportsman," recalled Laura Halpin as she sat in her Bainbridge farmhouse. "He loved the outdoors, and he hated deer-jackers. Some nights he went up into the tower to have a little fun with them. When he dropped the trap door the whole tower shook and echoed. He could hear the jackers scrambling through the woods to get away as fast as they could. Harry would then have a big laugh. He could entertain himself without too much trouble."

From 1949 to 1950, Laura, her husband and two sons lived in a three-room cabin at the base of the tower. "It had beautiful white pine walls and an oak floor. My husband and I used the bedroom in the back and my young son, Fay, slept in a crib in the pantry. My older son, Roy, slept on a day bed in the combination living room, kitchen and dining room," remembers Laura. "It was nice and comfortable. It was like being on a vacation."

Life in the cabin lacked conveniences. There was no electricity, so observers used kerosene lamps for lighting. A wood stove heated the cabin and was used for cooking.

"Our refrigeration was under the pantry floor," recalls Laura, "in an insulated wooden box lined with sawdust. We placed a 50-pound cake of ice in the box. We replaced it about twice a week. I kept my perishables such as meat, milk and my baby's formula in it.

"One day I heard a stone hit the roof of the cabin, and I rushed out to the porch. I could see my husband in the cab of the tower motioning to the stairs." At the fourth level of stairs, about 30 feet up, was Fay, her youngest son, leaning over the edge of the platform. "He said, 'Hi, mama.' I didn't dare to holler. All I could do was talk to him. Meanwhile, my husband was inching his way down the tower as I slowly climbed the stairs. He finally reached him and lifted him to safety."

The observers did have one convenience--a telephone. The cabin and the tower both had one. Observers had to maintain the telephone line to the tower because storms sometimes damaged the wires. From 1951 to 1960, Page Pond fire observers called in 136 fires.

* * *

"The fire tower and cabin are wonderful educational tools," comments Ed Engelman. "You can take campers to the top of the tower and see different species of trees budding out in spring and see the pattern they make on the landscape. They can also watch birds migrate. It opens the kids' eyes to new vistas." Since the Page Pond tower is on private land it is not open to the public. "We have to do it as a security measure for the users of the Girl Scout camp and to protect the tower from vandalism," says Engleman.

Page Pond Fire Tower and cabin are owned by the Girl Scouts Indian Hills Council, Inc., Binghamton, N.Y.
Ryan Podskoch

Observers

Emmett McDonald (1936-38), Lawrence Ryan (1939-1942), J. M. Slither (1942-44), Douglas E. Cable (1945), Richard Pratt (1946-48), Harry C. Halpin (1949-50?), Jesse Rockwell (1953-?), Franklin Phelps (1966?-79), Thomas Vroman (1970), not staffed (1971), Joe Cammer (1971), Tom Murphy (late 1970s), Jim Bagley (?), Jerra Fuller(?), Gary Moore (1988).

Rangers

William Gould (1935-1953), Ward Bradish (1955), Ed Wright (1957-1979), Charles Hurtgum (1969-88).

18. Petersburg Mountain, 1940

History

ACCORDING TO Schoharie County historian Wally Van Houten, "The state and CCC workers built Petersburg Mountain Fire Tower in 1940 near the hamlet of Patria in the Town of Fulton. The elevation of the mountain is about 2,311 feet and the tower was 68 feet high."

The CCC workers came from camp #S-93 in Break-abeen. They also built a cabin, constructed a 2-1/2 mile road and installed a telephone line for the tower. During the 1941 season, the observer spotted seven fires and registered 223 visitors. In 1952, 24 fires were spotted, and 404 visitors registered.

The area near the tower was used for recreation, especially for family picnics. In 1957, there were four fireplaces, six picnic tables and two toilets.

Retired Forest Ranger Gerald Hamm recounts one tragic event at the Petersburg tower. "One day, a young girl was crawling up the stairs of the tower. When she reached the second landing, she kept on going and fell off. The tragic accident prompted the state to secure turkey wire on the railings. Before this, there were large openings between the hand rail and the stairs."

The state also required signs to be placed at each tower recommending that children not climb the steps. The local ranger and observer recommended a minimum age of 15 for all visitors climbing the Petersburg tower.

At the end of the 1971 season, the DEC closed the Petersburg tower, and the following year placed it on the list of towers for disposal. Robert "Bucky" Williams, the regional forester, wrote in a report, "The above decisions are based on the assumption that aerial detection will continue at its present level." After the State closed the tower, Schoharie County took over

Petersburg Mountain Fire Tower was converted to a radio tower by Schoharie County. Ryan Podskoch

In 1971, the DEC closed the Petersburg Mountain Fire Tower and removed the lower stairs. Forest Ranger J. Graves is by the east side of the tower.
DEC files

Forest Ranger Gerald Hamm of Middleburgh supervised the Petersburg and Leonard Hill Fire Towers in Schoharie County.
Janice Hamm

ownership, removed the cab and extended the height of the tower for use as an emergency radio tower. Says Van Houten, "The cabin in which the observers lived was removed and the picnic tables and fireplaces are gone."

In 1999, Schoharie County removed the tower and a new tower was built to improve communications. The old tower was given to Al Moulin of Esperance who hopes (1999) to install it on his property.

Lore

RETIRED FOREST RANGER GERALD HAMM of Middleburgh has many stories about the Petersburg Mountain Fire Tower. An older woman, Leona Borst, was the observer from 1951 to 1971, and says Hamm, "I would hear the static of my radio, and then I'd hear Leona's concerned voice. 'Gerald, where are you?' Then a pause. 'Gerald, where are you? We need you.' I answered her, and she told me that she saw smoke and that I should get there as soon as possible."

Trouble for Hamm arose because Leona's voice was heard throughout the state. Hamm added, "When Leona saw a fire or smoke, she almost pleaded with you because she was so concerned about the fire. She had this sexy, sexy voice. So the rangers around the state were very jealous about me and Leona because she was always talking to me in a personal way. But Leona was

a lot older than I was and quite a stout woman. She was like my mother and always worried about where I was."

When Gerald went to a rangers' meeting, the rangers asked him about Leona. "All the rangers in the state knew her voice, and I never let on what Leona was really like," chuckles Gerald.

Retired Forest Ranger Pete Rossi recalls how Gerald's dog, George, always wanted to go with his master: "Gerald would rush to his truck and speed down his road. As he slowed down near a turn in the road, George, who was running after his truck, would climb the embankment near the curve. Just as the truck slowed for the curve, the dog would leap through the air and land on the cab. George held on to the roof, and his paws clung to the dome light. It was an unbelievable sight to see."

"George always rode on the cab of my truck. He couldn't fit in the back because of the Indian tanks and fire fighting equipment," says Hamm. "Once I was speeding to a fire about 75 miles an hour. A woodchuck ran across the road in front of me, and I had to slam on my brakes. George flew off the truck and rolled across the pavement, and I came to a screeching halt. He got back on his feet and jumped back on my truck. George just loved to ride with me."

* * *

Leona Borst's husband, Bob, liked to help maintain the grounds at the tower even though he was blind. Leonard Hill tower observer Luis Flores remembers: "I used to go to Leona's tower, and you wouldn't believe how great Bob kept the grass mowed. He used a heavy, hay rope to guide his lawn mower. Then he'd move the rope the width of his mower and mow back the other side. The lawn would be immaculate."

Bob helped Leona in many ways in spite of his handicap. He climbed the high tower each day at noon and brought up her lunch. He also did a lot of the cooking. Hamm adds, "If you wondered how she could stay up there all day, well, she would carry a large coffee can with her each day."

Bob and Leona used to stay at the cabin from early spring to the fall. Claudette Van Wie Wood of Middleburgh says, "My father, Claude Van Wie, was the ranger who supervised the tower. My dad and I would go up and stay at the cabin when Leona was away. I was about 11 years old, and I just loved to stay there. I can still remember the great view from the cab of the tower. It was remote, and the forest was beautiful."

Observers

Stanley Earles (1942-1943), Albert Tripp (1944-45), Philip W. Davis (1946-48), Robert Conrow (1948-1950), Leona Borst (1951), Douglas Mapes (1951), Leona Borst (1952-54), Clarence Loucks (1955), Leona Borst (1956-71).

Rangers

Claude Van Wie (1944-51), Herbert Brown (1952-55), Gerald Hamm (1955, 1958-69), John Graves (1970-77).

Directions

From Cobleskill, go south on Route 7 to Warnerville and take Route 4 east. Go up the mountain on West Fulton Road for about 2.9 miles. Turn left on Greenbush Road and go 0.6 of a mile. Then turn right on the dirt road called Head Road. Go 1.9 miles and on the left is the unmarked Tower Road. This road goes 0.4 of a mile to the tower.

From Delhi take Route 10 north to Route 7. Then go to Warnerville and follow the directions above.

From Middleburgh or Gilboa, take Route 30 to the West Fulton Road. Go 5.7 miles, turn right on Greenbush Road and follow the directions as above.

Forest Ranger Gerald Hamm's wife, Janice, brought her new baby, Kim, to Petersburg Fire Tower to see observer Leona Borst and her husband, Bob.
Gerald Hamm

19. Leonard Hill, 1948

History

IN 1947, the Conservation Department took down the 80-foot tower that stood at the Gilbert Lake State Park in Otsego County and rebuilt it on Hubbard Hill (2,630 feet) in the town of Broome in southeastern Schoharie County. The mountain is named after the Hubbard family, who have owned land and farmed there since the 1800s. However, the state misnamed it Leonard Hill Fire Tower, after a lower hill owned by Doctor Duncan Leonard next to Hubbard Hill. "It wasn't supposed to be Leonard Hill," says Frances Hubbard. Somebody got the maps mixed up. It always bothered me."

"Hubbard Hill was chosen as the site for the fire tower to protect 30,000 acres of state forest lands. It contained many trees planted in the 1930s by the CCC boys," says retired Forest Ranger Gerald Hamm of Middleburgh. "The fire tower had one of the best views in the state. It looked up many of the valleys of Schoharie County, such as Cole Hollow, the West Fulton Valley, Jefferson, and Grand Gorge."

In August 1946, the Conservation Department leased land for the fire tower from Clifton and Frances Hubbard. "Claude Van Wie, a forest ranger, and later sheriff of Schoharie County, worked with Ray Whitbeck in building the Leonard Hill Fire Tower," says Schoharie County historian, Wally Van Houten.

Fred H. VanAken was the first observer at the tower. He started working on April 8, 1949. He and other observers and the rangers parked at the Hubbard farm and followed a rugged trail along the telephone lines to the tower.

The state built a cabin at the base of the tower for observers. "I worked with Delhi forest ranger Noel Gonyo in the spring of 1949 for a couple of months to finish the cabin," says Dick Lewis, retired conservation officer from Gilboa.

"About 15 years after the tower was built, the state purchased about 75 acres of land from my parents," said Doug Hubbard, son of Clifton and Frances Hubbard. "The DEC built another road to the tower on the north side of the mountain, and we hardly ever saw the observers after that."

Retired ranger Peter Rossi says there has been much vandalism at the tower since it was closed in 1986: "I was called to the tower when fire was reported in the cab. When I got there, the floor of the cab was burned out."

Paul Trotta, supervising forester from the DEC office in Stamford, says, "There is no plan to sell Leonard Hill Fire Tower. I hope it will be saved because it is an historical landmark and a good focal point for the public to use for recreation. It would be good to rehabilitate it. We're looking to see if the public will come forward and ask to restore it."

Lore

OBSERVER LUIS FLORES grew up in Mexico. He read in the papers that American companies needed men because of the labor shortage due to Word War II. He says, "I was just a young punk, and I told my friends, 'Let's go for the physical test.' They said, 'No, we've got girl friends.' I told them that we would find new girls in America. So we got our physicals and got on a train.

"We traveled for days. I thought that we were going to California. Then the train stopped, and we were in Watkins Glen, New York. I met my wife there even though I didn't speak English and she didn't speak Spanish. We fell in love and were married within five months." They came back to his wife's hometown, Conesville. Luis worked at his father-in-law's sawmill and then switched to road construction.

In 1957, Luis became the observer at Leonard Hill Fire Tower. He says, "A man asked me if I wanted the job, but he added, 'If the political party in power changes, you'll have to change, too, if you want to keep the job.'"

Above: Observer Louis Flores (1957-64) sits in Leonard Hill Fire Tower looking out at southern Schoharie County and the northern Catskill Mountains. Luis Flores

Right: Peter Rossi supervised the Leonard Hill Fire Tower from 1972 to 1986. Peter Rossi

Below: Observer Luis Flores' family stayed at the cabin at Leonard Hill on weekends. Left to right: Sherry, Michael, Lori, Terry and Luis's wife, Eleanor. Luis Flores

Because Luis was a Republican, the man said that Luis would have to change parties if he wanted the job. Luis responded, "No. I can't. I can always find another job."

The next day another man, Charles Buel, came from the Conservation Department. He told Luis that he didn't have to change parties, and Luis got the job.

One day as Luis was walking to the tower from the Hubbard farm, he heard something following him. He says, "When I stopped, it stopped. When I started walking, it started. I said, 'Oh my God!' I really got shook up."

Luis ran up to the tower and into the cab. Looking down, he saw an animal. "It was a scrawny-looking fox, and it probably had rabies," says Luis. "Well, at the end of the day I ran as fast as I could down that hill to my truck. I then got a permit to have a gun, and I got a dog for protection."

"I used to have my family stay with me on the weekends," says Luis. "My two sons, Michael and Terry, and my two daughters, Sherry and Lori, had fun playing in the woods with my dog. My wife, Eleanor, brought the family up on Friday and stayed until Monday. Then we went home on Monday, my day off."

* * *

One observer stayed at the tower from the spring until the fall. Retired ranger Pete Rossi says, "Ken Greek was from Cobleskill. He and his wife stayed up at the tower because he didn't have a car. Whenever he needed a ride or groceries, a ranger would drive him. He enjoyed it up there. He even had his own vegetable garden."

Regional Ranger Ray Wood of New Paltz remembers an incident while working near Leonard Hill in 1966: "The State told the observers to leave their post in the tower whenever there was a threat of lightning. Well, Ken Greek thought up an idea for staying up in the tower during a thunder storm. He put a half-inch thick rubber mat on the floor of the cab and said, 'Now I'll be protected.' Ken waited for about two months for a good storm and finally the lightning did come," remembers Ray.

"My God, I'm safe, right here in the middle of all this lightning. I'm insulated, and I'm safe," said Greek to Ranger Wood.

"Well, he came down from the tower and told everyone about this insulating pad that he had on the floor and what a wonderful job it had done for him. Then about two days later," chuckled Ray, "all of his hair started to fall out in gobs. I'm sure that lightning had something to do with it. So after that, insulated pad or not, Ken never stayed up in the tower during a lightning storm. I think he learned a lesson."

"Ken Greek really knew a lot about nature and the surrounding area," says Ranger Jerry Hamm. "The people who came to Leonard Hill enjoyed listening to Ken's stories. The DEC lost an important public relations spokesperson when they closed down the towers because the observers saw the public every day. The observers were also very helpful to the rangers because they helped the rangers clear trail and mark state forest land boundaries."

* * *

One day during the 1980s, observer Judy Kalney Merwin gazed out the Leonard Hill fire tower window at the beautiful valleys and woods of Schoharie County. A young couple standing next to her had hiked to the tower and were learning about the area. Judy pointed to the majestic Catskill Mountains to the south and the fertile Schoharie Valley to the north.

In the distance they could see a single-engine plane approaching the tower. As the plane got closer, they saw that it was pulling something. The young man said to his girlfriend, "Look! It has a sign."

The words were now visible: "WILL YOU MARRY ME?" The young woman's eyes filled with tears. She embraced him with a heartfelt, "Yes."

During the spring and the fall, Judy had a difficult time keeping warm in the tower. "I started a fire in a woodstove in the cabin. Then I turned on a kerosene stove in the tower to keep me warm. I got up about every 15 minutes and walked around to keep warm."

Judy was never bored. "I read or listened to the radio while I was on duty. I'm a loner and I liked the solitude," she says.

* * *

On one occasion Luis Flores was working with Ranger Gerald Hamm clearing truck trails. He says, "Gerald was a very tough guy but one time he got into trouble. He saw this porcupine and he chased after it with a small axe. After he swung at it, there were three quills stuck in his knuckles. He tried to cut them out with his knife but there were still stubs. I said, 'Hold still. I'll get them out with my teeth.' I pulled them out and we got help from the other ranger, Lester Rosa."

After a 30-year absence from the tower, Luis was very upset when he visited it in 1998: "My beautiful cabin was gone. The rangers had taken it down and removed the lower stairs of the tower a few years before because they were afraid that someone might be injured. All the wonderful memories of the nice people who used to visit me and invite me to dinner came to me. It is so sad that I'll never see them again."

✳ ✳ ✳

"When I stayed there with my wife and daughters, I had no problems with vandalism," says observer Don Dyson. "But when I wasn't there, people would break into the cabin. Some even pulled the steel gates down with their four-wheel-drive vehicles."

Observers

Fred VanAken (1949-50), Ray Schermerhorn (1951-52), tower closed 1953-56, Luis Flores (1957-64), Willard T. Folland (1964-65), Ken C. Greek (1966-1973), Donald Dyson (1974-75), Milton E. Hewett (1975), Donald Dyson (1976-80), Judy Kalney Merwin (1981-86); Cliff and Don Oakley (also worked on Merwin's days off).

Rangers

Claude Van Wie (1950-51), Herbert D. Brown (1952-54), Gerald Hamm (1956-70), Peter Rossi (1972-86).

Directions

From Grand Gorge: Take Route 30 north. Turn right on Route 990V and go 1.2 miles across the bridge over Schoharie Creek. Take the first left, onto Flat Creek Road. Go about 7.1 miles to Broome Center. At the intersection, turn right onto Leonard Hill Road and proceed on this dirt road for about 1.4 miles. You will see a sign for Leonard Hill State Forest on the right. You can park and take a pleasant two-mile hike on the dirt road or drive a four-wheel-drive vehicle to the tower. The road travels through a beautiful evergreen state forest.

From Middleburgh: Take Route 30 south to Breakabeen. Turn left on County Route 17. After passing a cemetery and going 1.2 miles, turn right on Keyser Kill Road. Go 5.6 miles to Broome Center. Turn left on Leonard Hill Road and follow the directions above.

The DEC closed the Leonard Hill Fire Tower in 1986. Vandals destroyed the floor of the tower cab with a fire. Presently it is not maintained by the DEC.
Marty Podskoch

20. Roosa Gap, 1948

History

THE CONSERVATION DEPARTMENT chose Roosa Gap Mountain (1,500 feet) in the town of Mamakating in Sullivan County as the site for a 47-foot fire tower because it provided an excellent view of the Shawangunk Mountains south of the High Point tower. On July 1, 1946, William W. Taylor, a resident of New York City, granted New York State the right to use his land to build the tower.

A three-room wooden cabin with an attached woodshed was built near the tower, and early observers usually stayed there overnight. Roosa Gap Fire Tower began operating in 1948.

The DEC closed the tower in 1971 and sold it to Rudy Stutzmann in 1982. Today the tower is fenced off and leased by Sullivan County's Department of Public Works. The county maintains the tower as a base for the radio antennas on top. These are used for emergency and police communication purposes in the southern part of the county.

Lore

RETIRED FOREST RANGER HERB LEPKE JR. remembers a time when Roosa Gap observer Bob Boyer smelled smoke but couldn't see it: "Bob left the tower to find the fire, but when he got back, the fire had almost burned up the cabin and his truck."

"A visiting observer tried to move my truck but broke the key off in the ignition," recalls Boyer of Ferndale. "The fire peeled the paint off one side of the truck. I was just lucky that I wasn't in the tower when the intense flames scorched the area. It was in the high 80s that day, but luckily the temperature dropped about 50 degrees, and a rain came that night and later turned to snow. We had about two inches of snow in the morning and that put out the fire.

"I remember one evening when I had a group of friends visiting me, and we were playing horseshoes near the cabin. I went to the outhouse, and while I was sitting, I heard this rattling sound down below in the hole. I thought, 'Oh no, a rattlesnake!' I pulled up my pants as fast as I could, and I flew out the door like a rocket. My friends were so surprised I was running. I ran into the cabin and grabbed my shotgun, but when I got back and searched, I couldn't find it."

Everyone who visited the tower received a little talk about the mountains, forests, animals and plants. "Every observer," says Boyer, "was self-educated. He could talk about the herbs, wildlife and the importance of preventing fires."

* * *

The first fire tower observer was George Maier of Wurtsboro. "George loved the outdoors, and he loved his job even though it lacked some necessities," recalls his brother Ed. "He had to carry up five-gallon milk cans of water. There was no electricity so he stored his food in a little root cellar in the cabin floor. You could take out this board and reach down and keep your food and water at ground temperature."

* * *

Ed Maier says he liked to visit his brother during the fall. "It was gorgeous. With glasses on a clear day my brother said he could see the George Washington Bridge."

* * *

Ed Paige Jr. of Westbrookville remembers how his dad, Edwin Sr., appreciated nature: "He was never bored when he was up in the tower. He was a naturalist, and he enjoyed watching the migration of the monarch butterflies and birds as they flew near the tower."

During the 1940 and '50s, many fires in the area were caused by the New York, Ontario & Western

Above, left: The Roosa Gap Fire Tower can be seen from Route 209 near the Wurtsboro Airport. It is painted red and white and is off to the left of the airport. Marty Podskoch

Above: Bob Boyer was the observer at Roosa Gap from 1967-70. Marty Podskoch

Left: The observer's cabin. Ed Maier

Below: George Maier and his dog in front of the Roosa Gap cabin in 1949. After being the observer from 1949 to 1952, George became the local forest ranger. Ed Maier

Railway (O&W). "Many people called it the 'Old and Weary'" remembers Ed Maier, who ran a garage in Summitville. "As the engine climbed the hill to the tunnel, it needed more fuel and hot cinders flew from the smokestacks and landed in the nearby woods. The trains didn't have screens on the stacks."

Maier adds, "I was a fire warden, and in 1947 there were about 500 fire wardens in District 13, which had its headquarters in Middletown. We were volunteers interested in the welfare of our community. The Conservation Department paid us 50 cents an hour for fighting fires. The rangers had the power to call upon any able-bodied person to fight a fire. If a person refused to help and didn't have a good reason, he could be taken to court and charged with a misdemeanor."

Ed Maier fought many fires on the Shawangunk Mountains with Indian tanks. "They contained five gallons of water. We used a hand pump to spray or squirt water on the fire. They could reach up to 25 or 30 feet ahead of you. You could knock a fire right down. I had a jeep that had a 55-gallon tank on the back. I could drive right along the railroad track while Floyd Budd, another local fire warden, would take a hose and put the fires out."

* * *

Floyd Budd, a retired carpenter from Phillipsport, recalls, "We were given a council rake that had cutters, or blades, from mowing machines. They were riveted onto the rake. You could cut a route off in the woods and make a fire break. You could cut laurel and brush

right down and have a path of dirt. We also used brown straw brooms with heavy bristle to sweep away debris."

* * *

In the fall of 1982, Rudy Stutzmann, a retired funeral director from Port Washington says, "While reading the *New York Times,* I saw an ad for a fire tower for sale. It also had a cabin and 151 acres of land. Well, I was familiar with the area as I had been flying since 1961 from the Wurtsboro Airport. The land was formerly owned by the New York City Boy Scouts and was then owned by a man from Michigan."

Stutzmann bought the land and paid the Conservation Department $100 for the tower and cabin. I told the state that I'd buy the tower if they took down the cabin because it was falling down," says Rudy, adding that he enjoys flying over his land and the Roosa Gap Fire Tower, his own bit of Shawangunk Mountain history.

Observers

George Maier (1949-52), Otto Schwarz (1953-54?), Edwin Paige (1963-1966), Robert Boyer (1967-70).

Rangers

George Maier (1953-57), Donald Decker (1958-62), John Gillen (1968-74).

21. Graham, 1949

History

ON JUNE 1, 1948, the Orange County Board of Supervisors approved $1,000 to move the Pocatello fire tower (elevation 830 feet) near Middletown to the Shawangunk Mountains. The 60-foot Aermotor Co. tower was set up on a ridge of the Shawangunk Mountains (elevation 1,310 feet) near Otisville. The new location was chosen because it covered not only the Middletown area but also the Town of Deerpark, the Neversink Valley from Port Jervis to Wurtsboro and the length of Oakland Valley.

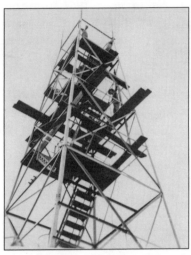

Conservation Department workers building the Graham Fire Tower near Otisville in 1949.

Captain Ray Wood

In August 1949, the Conservation Department received permission to put the tower on George S. Writer's property in the Town of Mount Hope. The Writer farmland was about three miles south of Otisville on County Route 73, Mountain Road.

The department also received an easement on land owned by Ernest Crine of Port Jervis for a road and telephone line to the tower site.

In 1977, the state attached a radio repeater to the fire tower to help with communications. The DEC closed Graham Fire Tower in 1988.

Lore

DURING THE 1980s, Forest Ranger Greg Wagner of Cuddebackville frequently visited Graham Fire Tower. Late one morning, he climbed tower when observer Donna Tunno was on duty. They sat at the circular map table and started eating their lunch. Greg looked out the windows to enjoy the panoramic view of the valleys to the east and west of the Shawangunk Mountains. He could even see the large stone tower of High Point, New Jersey, in the distance. Then he looked down the valley where Route 209 led to Port Jervis.

"Donna! Look at that huge cloud of white smoke toward Port Jervis! Get a reading from the map table and call the DEC office in New Paltz. I'm going now. Call me on the radio with the exact location" he directed.

Greg flew down the stairs, jumped in his truck, and sped down the dusty, serpentine road. Meanwhile, Donna was busy calling fire wardens in the Port Jervis area to meet Greg. Donna then coordinated the fire fighters from her post.

The fire got out of control due to extreme dryness and high winds. Ranger Wagner recalls, "After a few days of fighting the fire, we were exhausted. We had to bring 10 rangers from the Adirondacks to help us. They were surprised to see such large fires. Our boss, Captain Ray Wood, said, 'These guys are used to working in the *Asbestos Forest* of the north. They don't know what it's really like to fight fires.'" Eventually 1,800 acres were consumed by the brutal fire.

"Incendiaries were the biggest cause of fires," says Wagner. "There were a lot of fires in the Huguenot and Peenpack Trail area to the west of Route 209 near Port Jervis. Some said that the huckleberry pickers started the fires. Others said that the fires were set by men who needed money. If there was a fire, they would volunteer to fight the fire and be paid by the Conservation Department."

* * *

Left: Sharon Tunno Galligan was 18 years old when she succeeded her mother as the observer at Graham Fire Tower. *Above:* Fire warden Dave Brinckerhoff fought many fires in the Shawangunk and Catskill Mountains. *Below:* Graham Fire Tower and cabin in 1999. Marty Podskoch

Retired fire warden Dave Brinckerhoff remembers, "The railroad came from Narrowsburg to Port Jervis. The brakes threw off sparks that started fires, especially in the spring and fall, when it was dry."

Fires also started when sparks flew from burning rubbish. Shirley Hujus of Otisville remembers her husband giving fire permits. "People called if they were going to burn rubbish, and the observer was notified of its location. My husband was the acting fire chief, and he was also a fire warden. He fought many brush fires. Later, I was asked to take his job of issuing burning permits."

Brinckerhoff remembers another cause of fire: "I was working as a prison guard, and I was on vacation. The local ranger, Kenny Denk, asked me to work for two weeks at Graham. It was a dry summer, and I was busy calling in fires that started where they were building Route 84. They were burning a lot of brush and sometimes the fires spread."

Brinckerhoff remembers days when it was very hot: "We would carry Indian tanks filled with five gallons of water. Sometimes one guy carried a tank filled with three or four quarts of beer and ice to keep us cool."

* * *

Another Orange County fire warden, Jim Winterbottom, now of Canton, New York, remembers some humorous and scary times fighting fires: "One time we were fighting a fire near the winery in Washingtonville. The monks were so happy with our help that they had the planes drop us Indian tanks filled with wine bottles. We were higher than kites."

On another occasion, he relates, "We were fighting a fire that was really hard to get under control. They sent us planes from the Orange County Airport, and they carried 'wet water,' a fire retardant mixture. I saw the planes continuously missing the target so I got on the CB and said, 'You guys can't hit anything. I could do a better job.' Well, District Ranger Sid Bascomb heard me. He called me and said to come down and show the pilots how to do it better. When I got there, they were loading these old torpedo planes. I got into the front seat, and the pilot was behind me. We took off, and I started to get nervous. The pilot flew toward the fire, and we were so low I thought we were going to crash. I'll tell you, I didn't give a damn where he dropped the water. I looked for a parachute, and the pilot said, 'If you're thinking of jumping out, you don't have a chance. You'd be like a fly on the windshield if you jumped.' We were lower than the tree tops and dropped our load. As we started to climb up, the wings snapped off tree tops. Luckily the plane didn't crash, and that was the last time I ever complained about the pilot. Now you know why I have gray hair."

* * *

To help combat loneliness, observer Steve Canfield took his beagle to the tower for company. "The dog would climb the steps to the top of the tower and scratch at the trap door to be let in."

Observer Sharon Tunno took her cat with her: "He liked climbing the tower and keeping me company in the cab. Then he would go down and hunt all day and be waiting at my truck when it was time to go home."

* * *

Three women were observers at Graham. The first was Kim Chiperino. Later, Donna Tunno Fallon was hired. Ralph Tunno, a long-time volunteer fire fighter from Westbrookville, says, "My former wife, Donna, loved nature and liked her job as observer. My daughter Sharon took the job after Donna left."

"Both Donna and Sharon were terrific. They were dedicated and good at spotting fires," says ranger Greg Wagner. "You never had to worry about them being at their post."

* * *

Observer Donna Tunno Fallon says, "I had a lot of visitors. Some rode their horses from the local riding stables. We would show them how we used the map and range finder to locate fires. We also talked about our weather station."

* * *

Observer Canfield recalls painting the tower. "Ranger John Gillen and I would stick boards out the windows so that we could paint the roof. We lashed the boards to the map table that was in the middle. Then I'd climb out and paint the roof with a roller."

Canfield says, "One day when I was walking, a rattlesnake rapped me in my boot. It left a two-pronged mark in the leather with venom dripping down."

One observer, who wishes to remain anonymous, found rattlesnakes to be profitable. "We were getting one or two snakes a week. We put them in a milk jug and froze them. Some snakes were six feet long and we would get two dollars a foot for them."

Few people in the Middletown area are aware that this historical site exists. "It's sad to see the fire towers closed," says Ralph Tunno. "They are an important part of our history. They should be preserved."

Observers

W. G. Smith (1949-52), Charles R. O'Neill (1953-54?), Otis Meade (1957-?), Dave Brinckerhoff (a substitute, 1966 or '67), Charles Houghtaling (1967?-69) Steve Canfield (1970-71?), ? Messeros (?), Charlie Smith (?), Kim Chiperino (?), Steve Bazan (?), Dane Wagner (?), Robert Herberger (?), Donna Tunno Fallon (?), Sharon Tunno Galligan (1988).

Rangers

Earl Brewer (1948-61), Bill Morse (1961-64), Kenneth Denk (1967-69), Charles Hurtgam (1969-73), Greg Wagner (1974-88)

Graham Fire Tower
Marty Podskoch

22. Overlook Mountain, 1950

History

GALLIS HILL FIRE TOWER was removed from the Kingston area in 1950 by Conservation Department workers and moved eight miles north of the village of Woodstock, where it was rebuilt on Overlook Mountain (3,140 feet). This new location gave a commanding vista of the eastern Catskills.

The state received an easement from landowner Wilbert D. Newgold to build the tower, cabin, telephone line and truck road from Mead Mountain Road to the summit.

Observer Barnet "Barney" Howland and rangers Frank Borden, Aaron Van De Bogart and Herb Lepke Sr. helped move the 60-foot tower. Howland says, "We used a bulldozer to widen the old road that used to go to the old Overlook Mountain House. Then we built the tower and cabin. I loved my job, but I had to give it up to get a better-paying job so I could send my daughter to college."

The tower began operating in 1951, and Barney Howland reported seven fires, followed by 23 fires in 1953 and four fires in 1954.

After 37 years service the DEC closed Overlook Mountain Fire Tower in 1988. "I was sad to see the tower closed down because the fire observers were very good at teaching the hikers about fire safety and ecology," said retired Forest Ranger Roger Blatter of West Hurley.

Lore

OVERLOOK MOUNTAIN offers one of the best views of the Catskills. According to Blatter: "From the tower or from the ledges, the hiker has a panoramic view of the Berkshire Mountains, the Hudson River, the Ashokan Reservoir, the Shawangunk and the Catskill Mountains. You can see seven states."

"Johnny Baldwin was one of the observers at Overlook," says Blatter. "He was great with the hikers at the tower, but he wanted to keep it in good shape. Well, word got out that he was strict."

Baldwin chuckles, "Sometimes I had trouble with some of the hikers and campers who wanted to break into my cabin by the tower. I learned how to catch rattlesnakes from Ranger Aaron Van De Bogart and people knew this. Well, I used to keep a black snake in my cabin to deal with rodents, and sometimes it would crawl up on the chair and peer out the window. The hikers would see this and word got out that there was a rattlesnake in the cabin. After that, I had no problem with people trying to break into my cabin."

"I also had a tame deer and a tame bear cub that I called Tedra," says Baldwin. "One summer Tedra got lost, and I looked for about a week. One day I heard some people screaming and I rushed to see what was the matter. I saw Tedra at the base of a tree going through some backpacks. Two hikers were clinging to the top of the tree screaming for help. When I got to Tedra, she jumped up into my arms. The hikers couldn't believe their eyes, and reluctantly climbed down after I told them that she was tame."

Baldwin liked to have fun with the hikers. Sometimes he would bet the visitors that he could climb up the tower on the outside steel bars faster than they could using the stairs. "They thought it was impossible, so they'd start climbing up the stairs and I started on the outside," says Baldwin. "They would stop on the stairs and look at me in amazement. While they stared at me, I made it to the top before they did."

One time Baldwin was searching for an airplane that went down in a storm. "When the plane crashed, it hit a maple tree and a branch pierced the body of the

Facing page, above: **View of the Catskill Mountains from Overlook Mountain Fire Tower. Overlook Mountain House is on the right; the Ashokan Reservoir is in the distance.** Captain Ray Wood Collection

Below: **An aerial photo by the author.**

Above: John Baldwin served as observer at the Overlook Fire Tower from 1962 to 1988. Marty Podskoch

Left: Ranger Frank Borden, standing on the tower, helped in the construction. DEC and Captain Ray Wood

Below: Barney Howland is loading a dump truck with gravel. Mount Tremper observer Harry Baldwin is standing near the truck. Captain Ray Wood Collection

plane and went up between the pilot's legs and went right through his arm muscle," remembers Baldwin. "He sat in the plane all night looking at the lightning and thunder storm. When we found him the next day, we had to saw the branch above and below his arm to get him out. He was thankful to God that he didn't die."

Of about 18 plane crash searches, this was the only victim that Baldwin found alive. Most of the time the searchers put Vicks by their nostrils because the stench of decaying flesh was unbearable. "On one occasion we were with a trooper, and we could smell something awful, and we told the trooper that the crash was ahead. He said, 'Stand back; I'll check it out first to see if there are any survivors.' Well, he went over and started throwing up. That's why you'll never catch me flying," says Baldwin.

* * *

Aaron Van De Bogart supervised the Overlook Tower from 1950 to 1971. Retired Forest Ranger Bill Morse says, Aaron was a real woodsman. He loved to catch rattlesnakes. He had them in a large tank, which he kept in his house. Well, one day he decided to clean the tank. He let them out in his lawn. Shortly after, a guy drove up with a load of dog food. He started walking across the lawn and Aaron yelled, 'Hey, watch out for my friends!' The man looked down into the grass and saw the rattlesnakes slithering toward him. Well, the man threw the food into the air and ran for his truck in a flash. That was the last time he made a delivery to Van De Bogart's house."

Forest Ranger Aaron Van De Bogart supervised Mount Tremper and Overlook Fire Towers, 1942, 1945-71.
Jane Van De Bogart

Aaron's wife, Jane, of Woodstock says, "Aaron loved animals. He would bring orphaned animals back to our house. We had snakes, a fawn and even a bear. One day the bear was outside and walked over to the neighborhood children who were waiting for their school bus. He went up to them and ran off with their lunches. Aaron realized that we could no longer keep it. He hated to give it up, but he had to."

Observers

Barnet Howland (1950-54), Jack Sylvester (1960s), John Baldwin (1962-88).

Rangers

Aaron Van De Bogart (1942, 1945-71) Roger Blatter (1972-88).

Directions

Two trails lead to the fire tower. To find the more popular one, start at the Village Green in Woodstock and drive north on Rock City Road. At the stop sign, Rock City becomes Meads Mountain Road; proceed up this steep road for 2.5 miles. The state parking lot and trailhead are on the right. The 2.5-mile trail ascends gradually but at times becomes strenuous.

When you are almost at the fire tower, you will see a four-story concrete wall ahead, the remains of Overlook Mountain House. Thousands of people stayed at the first Overlook Mountain House in the late 1800s, including President Ulysses S. Grant. This hotel burned in 1875, was rebuilt, and burned again in 1924. Today's concrete walls were poured in 1928. The project was abandoned with the onset of World War II.

"I've hiked Overlook hundreds of times; in my younger days I would run up and down the mountain," says Bill Spangenberger, an avid hiker and founder of the 3500 Club. In his nineties at the turn of the century, he continues hiking and playing tennis.

A second trail begins from the north at Platte Clove, where County Route 16 and Prediger Road meet, but is longer (approximately 6 miles) and less frequently used. Take the Devil's Path (red) Trail 1.9 miles to the Overlook (blue) Trail. From there, it is 4.0 miles to the tower.

23. Bramley Mountain, 1950

History

In 1950, the DEC built an Aermotor Co. 80-foot tower on Bramley Mountain (2,817 feet) six miles north of Delhi in Delaware County. The observer could see Mount Utsayantha in Stamford and the Rock Rift Fire Tower 10 miles south of Walton.

Bramley tower was built during the postwar period with Federal Capital Reconstruction Funds. The state received a right-of-way from Harlon Briscoe of Bovina to build a telephone line and a road to the summit. Briscoe leased the land to the state.

Ranger Lester Rosa and Utsayantha observer Jim Davies built a three-room, pine-paneled observer's cabin, and local electric and telephone companies strung lines to the tower and cabin. Later, the Delaware County Electric Cooperative built a radio antenna for communication purposes about 60 feet from the tower.

After it had been in service for about 20 years, the DEC closed the Bramley tower at the end of 1970. In 1975 the state sold the tower to Pete Clark of Delhi for $50.

Lore

In 1952, Therese "Que" Aitken from Bovina was one of the few female observers in New York State. "I've always loved nature," comments Therese. "When I heard that there was an opening for a fire tower observer's job, I went to Hobart to see Dr. Bush, who was a dentist and a politician. He said, 'I guess it's OK.' So I got the job."

"The state had a hard time getting people to work at Bramley tower because it was so high. Many people quit when they got to the second or third landing," remembers Ranger Lester Rosa of Arkville.

The road up the mountain to the tower was very rough. However, Therese was able to get Clayton Thomas to fix up a Model T Ford that would get her to the tower.

Therese started her job at about nine in the morning and worked till about six in the evening. "When I got to the cab of the tower, I called the Delhi operator to see if my telephone was working," says Terese. Noel Ganyo from Delhi was one of the forest rangers in charge of the tower. Either he or a fire warden was notified when smoke was spotted.

Therese says her job had some fringe benefits: "I had two boys who were in 5th and 6th grade, and I would take them to the tower on weekends. Sometimes they brought their friends to play cowboys and Indians while I was up in the tower. I had a good vantage point from which to watch them. They would bring their sleeping bags and sleep in the cabin."

* * *

Stella McPherson and her kindergarten class from Andes visited the Bramley Mountain fire tower on October 19, 1968. Here are some of the students' comments about their visit:

"It was fun!"
"I like it."
"It was cool!"
"I ate six hot dogs."
"Let's do it again."
"Thank you, Mr. Atken. It was perfect."

Comments like these are in the old register that used to be at the base of the fire tower. The register was saved by Jim Andrews of Andes, a neighbor of Chuck Atken, who was a long-time fire observer on Bramley Mountain. Andrews recalls: "Four or five families used to go at least once a year to 'Chuck's Tower.' We would load everyone into a neighbor's truck and drive up. There was a picnic table and a fireplace, where we could

Facing page: **The Bramley Mountain Fire Tower, located north of the Village of Delhi in Delaware County, was in operation from 1951-1970.** DEC file photo -Ranger Captain Pat Kilpeck

cook hot dogs and hamburgers. We thought it was great. The views were spectacular. Once, when we were there, Chuck spotted an actual fire, and that was exciting."

Andrews also has vivid memories of the observer's cabin: "Chuck's wife, Vi, furnished the cabin. She had great taste. There were a couple of easy chairs and a braided rug on the floor. The cookstove was always well polished and warmed the cabin during our fall visits."

Every visitor was impressed by the way Chuck maintained the fire tower grounds. "He kept the lawns mowed and made trails to some ledges behind the cabin. We had fun crawling into the caves and playing around the summit," says Andrews.

* * *

Evelyn and Howard Gerken owned a farm near Bramley Mountain. "I remember taking our family to the tower in the summer. Howard drove us up in his truck," says Evelyn.

"Chuck Atken kept the tower in good shape. It was a show-place. He kept the grass mowed and kept the road up," says Howard Gerken.

After working 12 years at Bramley Tower, Atken continued to work for the Conservation Department helping at Little Pond and doing trail work. He died in 1972. "We loved Chuck. He was a gentleman and a great outdoorsman," says Ranger Gerald Hamm of Middleburgh.

* * *

After closing the tower in the fall of 1970, the DEC put it up for sale. "Dick Wilbur worked at the Conservation Office and he told me about the sale," recalls Pete Clark, a dairy farmer from Elk Creek Road near Delhi. "I bought the tower for $50. My brother Dave and I loved to visit the tower and thought it would be nice to put the tower up on our hill."

Jim Andrews remembers seeing the tower while the Clarks were taking it down: "I can remember going back to college and traveling past Harold Cole's Silver Lake, on Route 28. You could always see it [Bramley Mountain Fire Tower] from the road, but this day I

looked over and saw only half of the tower. I told my dad that it looked really strange."

It took the Clarks four days to take the tower down. "When you're taking it down, you're working with nothing around you. It got quite shaky when we took the steps down," says Dave Clark.

The stairs and cab were placed in one of Pete Clark's barns and the galvanized steel beams near his machine shed. Each piece is color-coded with paint. "I made some sketches of the tower and marked the galvanized steel beams so that we could put it back together. I still have the plans," says Dave Clark.

The tower was never rebuilt because the Clarks worried about liability problems in the event someone was injured on their property.

In the fall of 1997, a group of Delhi and Bovina residents formed the Bramley Mountain Fire Tower Club with the purpose of placing the fire tower back on Bramley Mountain. Their goal is to purchase the land and rebuild the tower on its original site. The group is also seeking a right-of-way on the road that runs from Bramley Mountain Road to the summit. Currently (2000) the land is owned by John Tara.

The Clarks told the club that they would be willing to give up the tower so that it could be restored. "I guess it would be nice to have it back in its original location so that my children and grandchildren could hike to the tower and enjoy the beautiful views," says Pete Clark. "The whole community would benefit."

The tower was a landmark for many people. "My family enjoyed hiking to the tower several times a year," says Vi Laing, who raised seven children at the foot of Bramley Mountain. "You could see all the way to the fire tower from the top of Meridale Mountain. On our way home from Oneonta, my kids would say, 'Mom, we're almost home. There's the fire tower.'"

Once the land is purchased and the tower rebuilt, the observer's cabin will be restored, possibly as an interpretive museum, where fire tower memorabilia could be displayed, or as a residence for a guide, who could tell visitors about local ecology and the history of the fire tower. Guides might be recruited from SUNY Delhi's Parks & Recreation program and its Americorps program. Similar programs are in place at some of the restored Adirondack fire towers.

"The community has been very supportive of the project, and we hope to have children and adults hiking again and enjoying the beautiful views of our Catskill Mountains," comments Tim Bray, a member of the Bramley Mountain Fire Tower Club.

Observers

Ernest Jackson (spring 1951), Therese Aitkins (1952), tower closed (1953-57?), Charles Atken (1958-70).

Rangers

Noel Ganyo (1951-69), Peter Rossi (1970-71).

Left, top: **Evelyn Gerkin, Jinny Smith and Gerry Downey visit the tower.** Evelyn Gerkin

Left: **Bramley Mountain observer Chuck Atken (1958-70) and his wife, Vi, stand by the tower.** Jim Andrews

Above, top: **Jim Andrews of Andes signs the guest register at the foot of Bramley Tower.** Jim Andrews

Above: **Forest Ranger Lester Rosa worked at many fire towers in Ulster and Delaware Counties.** Lester Rosa

Airplane Surveillance Replaces Fire Towers

History

IN 1969, the DEC experienced budget cuts and decided to experiment with airplane surveillance to detect fires. In the fall of 1970, eight contracts were awarded to patrol the southern part of the state. The contracts were extended into 1971. Contractors flew specific routes when weather conditions were hot, dry and windy. The state expected to save money by reducing the number of fire towers and observers.

In 1971, the DEC contracted for 22 experimental flights state-wide, five of which covered the Catskill region. When the danger of fire was high, district forest rangers notified the pilots to fly. The saving were substantial: $250,000 in 1972.

As a result of using air surveillance, the state closed 61 of the 102 fire towers. Captain Ray Wood, DEC regional forest ranger in New Paltz, says, "In 1971 we closed seven fire towers in our district, including Mohonk and Mount Tremper in the Catskill region. We kept only the following five towers open: Red Hill, Balsam, Overlook, Graham and Sterling." In 1975, says Charles Boone, superintendent of forest fire control in Albany, 22 flight loops discovered 795 uncontrolled fires that burned 2,968 acres.

According to Ranger Wood, "In 1986 the state cut the number of flights and started to phase out the use of airplanes. By 1987 the DEC had concluded that the job of aircraft patrols and fire towers had been taken over by the public. Citizens called in 82 percent of the forest fires in the state while fire tower observers spotted only about 4 per cent of the fires."

There were many reasons for this change. More people had moved into the Catskills, and when they spotted smoke, they notified rangers and local fire departments. Fewer fires occurred because the leading causes of fires were almost totally eliminated. Railroads declined and what few trains remained caused fewer fires. Strict ordinances eliminated the burning of fields and rubbish. Berry pickers, who used to start fires to improve the crop, stopped picking. The Smokey the Bear program and improved fire safety awareness resulted in fewer careless fires.

By 1990, the DEC had stopped using both aircraft patrols and staffed fire towers in New York State. An important era in New York State conservation came to a conclusion. The men and women in the lofty fire towers, who faithfully scanned the forests for smoke, were eliminated. The pilots who bravely guided their small airplanes through intense heat, winds, fog and storms lost an extra source of income.

Northeast Catskills

During the 1970s and early 80s, Gale Brownlee flew her Cessna 206 and patrolled the northeastern part of the Catskills searching for puffs of smoke. Gale worked for Hank Cramer, manager and pilot of Carroll Air Service at the Kingston-Ulster Airport.

The U. S. Weather Service in Albany issued daily fire reports; usually in the spring and fall when there was a high risk of forest fires. A Class 1 day meant the least dangerous, a Class 5 day meant the greatest threat of fire.

Brownlee says, "The DEC would notify my boss, Hank Cramer, to patrol the Catskills. When I got a call about 8 A.M. I knew that it was Hank calling for me to fly."

Cramer had two flights. "The Columbia Route" flew the eastern side of the Hudson River. Brownlee flew the 120-mile "Greene Route," north along the western side of the Hudson River to Albany County and then south to Greene and northern Ulster Counties. In Ulster County she flew to Pine Hill and southeast to the Ashokan Reservoir and back to the airport in Kingston.

Her 120-mile circuit flight took about an hour and a half. Sometimes she flew three or four loops a day. Her flight covered about 70,000 acres of state park land: 650 square miles in Greene County, 206 square miles

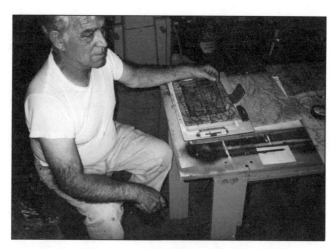

Above, left: Pilot Marcel Thompson looking at his map of the Catskills showing the three routes he patroled during the 1970s. Marty Podskoch *Above, right:* Don Beaudin, who owned the Westville Airport near Cooperstown, had the State contract to patrol the north and western Catskills. Gail Beaudin Pierce *Below:* Pilot Gale Brownlee preparing to take off from the Kingston Airport. Gale Brownlee

Tony Barone, owner of the Wurtsboro Airport,
patrolling the southern Catskill Mountains
looking for forest fires.
George Barone

Marcel Thompson in a Cessna 172 he flew patrolling
the northwest Catskills searching for smoke
during the 1970s and 1980s.
Marcel Thompson

in Schenectady County, 526 square miles in western
Albany County, and 286 square miles in Ulster
County.

Gale flew her plane at about 6,000 feet patrolling
for smoke. Sometimes she dropped to 2,000 feet or
lower to get a closer look at a suspected fire.

While flying she had to look at her maps and
pinpoint the fire and use a grid locator. Then she called
the nearest fire tower observer on her radio. The observer then called the district forest ranger, Victor
Schrader of Catskill. Schrader called local fire fighters
and forest rangers to extinguish the blaze.

Originally a model in New York City and California, Brownlee came back to her hometown of Woodstock in 1959. "I wanted to do something different,"
she says. "An ad in the paper for a free flying lesson
caught my attention. I tried it and loved it. I borrowed
money from the bank and bought my own plane." Gale
got her commercial license in 1964 and became a flight
instructor and won a scholarship for flying helicopters
in 1965.

"Most of the fires were caused by humans, usually
from campfires," she says. "Sometimes the sun shining
through a discarded bottle along the road or in the
woods could start a fire. I would call the ranger and
many times I could lead them right to the fire since they
could not see over the trees. I adored my job because I
was protecting my mountains. In the spring and fall
when the leaves are very dry or not there, mountains

look like purple elephants as far as you can see. I love
them."

Southeast Catskills

Tony Barone, owner of the Wurtsboro Airport, was
awarded contracts to fly three routes in the southern
Catskill Mountains and the area extending to the Pennsylvania border. Tony's son, George, remembers patroling the region: "The Tango Run" started from our
airport. First we flew to Red Hill near Claryville, then
on to Balsam Lake Mountain, then over Belleayre and
Mount Tremper, then over the Ashokan Reservoir to
Mohonk. We would follow the ridge of the Shawangunk Mountains and back to Wurtsboro."

The second run was called the "Whiskey Run."
The pilot followed Route 209 to Port Jervis then went
up the Delaware River to Sky Top and over to Livingston Manor. On the return trip the pilot followed
Route 17 back to the Wurtsboro Airport.

The "Uniform Run" was the third run. "I would
fly down toward Newburgh and Stewart Airport," says
George Barone. "I would also stay away from West
Point because there would be quite a few fires, and I
didn't have to worry about them. Then I flew down
Central Valley to Harriman Park where there was a
lake that was a check point. Then we flew back to
Wurtsboro."

Three pilots would patrol at the same time. George Barone and his father hired retired airline pilots to help them.

Northwest Catskills

In 1969 the Stamford, N.Y., DEC office started to study the idea of using airplanes to search for fires in the northern and western sections of the Catskills. Don Beaudin, owner of the Westville Airport south of Cooperstown, says, "I took District Forest Ranger Phil Carter up a few times in the fall of 1969. I showed him how a pilot could see a larger area than a single observer in a tower."

The fall foliage blazed in a kaleidoscope of bright colors as I flew over the Catskill Mountains in October 1997. I had hired pilot Art Smith of Oneonta to give me a bird's-eye view of the fire towers and the forests that they had protected. It was sad to see the desolate, rusting towers and empty cabins below. On Mount Tremper, for example, we flew around the summit five times before we spotted the rusted roof and frame of the abandoned fire tower.

Marcel Thompson, a pilot from Don Beaudin's airport, flew 184 flights and logged 644 hours patrolling the Catskills. He says, "On a clear day while flying at 8-10,000 feet, I could cover 10,000 square miles in a three-hour period. There were some observers who could see quite far. On a clear day Linda Trask, the observer at Rock Rift fire tower, could spot a fire up to 50 miles away. But I had the advantage over the observer in that I could fly right over the smoke. I could see if it was someone burning leaves, a barbecue grill, or a real forest fire."

Lore

ON A SCORCHING SUMMER DAY during the 1970s, Marcel Thompson was patrolling the western Catskills. He recalls it was one of the driest times that he had ever seen and fires were springing up everywhere. Flying south of Hancock near French Mountain Rd., he saw something very strange: There was a large fire on top of the hill. As I flew closer, I saw this guy running out of the woods and jumping into a light blue van."

Flying at a low elevation, Thompson couldn't contact any ranger with his state radio, so he used his airplane radio. He called the Broome County Airport in Binghamton and the airport relayed his message to the state police. They contacted the rangers and a coordinated chase ensued.

"I wound up following that guy down Route 17. I was about 100 feet above and slightly behind him," says Thompson. "He never knew I was there. We finally got him cornered just as he got into Liberty. There was a state trooper waiting for him. That fire damaged 500 acres of forest."

Thompson, a resident of Goodyear Lake, was born in France and came to the U. S. in 1951. After graduating from high school, he joined the Air Force and served in the Vietnam War. Later he earned an instructor's license for planes and gliders and taught for many years at the Westville Airport.

My "1 Bravo Route" started at Westville and I flew to Mount Utsayantha fire tower in Stamford," he explains. "I followed the West Branch of the Delaware River to Walton and the Rock Rift fire tower by the Cannonsville Reservoir. From there I flew over Downsville and Cat Hollow Road to Belleayre Mountain fire tower. My sixth check point was Gilboa and my last was back over Utsayantha. Then I would go back to Westville Airport."

Thompson and two other pilots patrolled three routes from about 1969 until about 1982. Each route took about three hours to complete. Sometimes, when it was very dry, a pilot flew a route two or three times in one day. Marcel says he flew three different routes in one day when they did not have enough pilots.

Flying in the Catskills could be very dangerous. "Sometimes the fog became so thick you couldn't see the mountains, recalls Marcel Thompson. "The winds could also be dangerous. There were a few times I was lucky to get out alive. One time the fog became so thick, I had to fly very low. The visibility was getting lower and lower. There were mountains on both sides of me and clouds above. There was maybe 200 feet of ground clearance and it was getting scary. I could not turn around. The turbulence was so severe that I had no control over the plane. Only once in a while could I nudge the plane where I wanted it to go. Luckily I made it back to the airport alive."

There was, however, one windy day that Marcel Thompson had a humorous experience while flying near Mount Utsayantha: "A strong south wind was blowing and I had a hard time flying against it. I flew into the wind toward the tower. I was just about moving. I gradually got closer and closer to the tower. When I got very close, I slowed down a bit and you should have seen the face on the fire tower observer. I was almost standing still in front of him. Finally, I turned away and I'm sure he was quite relieved."

The DEC called the second air route the "Alpha" or "Oneonta Route." Fred Purdy of Fort Plain usually flew this route. It started at Westville Airport and followed check points at Oneonta, Bainbridge, Davenport Center, West Fulton (Schoharie County), Leonard Hill fire tower (near Gilboa Dam), Lawyersville (west of Cobleskill) and back to Westville. This route flew mainly over the D. & H. Railroad tracks because some fires started from sparks from the hot brakes as the trains descended the hills.

From his home in Dunnellon, Florida, Don Beaudin remembers flying the third air route: "My route started at Westville and I flew toward Norwich. My check points were Sherburne, Hamilton, then south to Otselic, and the west side of Binghamton. Then I flew east to Long Eddy and up the Delaware River to Harpursville, Afton, Bainbridge, Norwich and back to Westville."

Beaudin secured the contract to patrol the western Catskills in his Cessna 172. He liked this plane because it had more room than a Skyhawk, and it flew faster and had greater range.

The ranger called Beaudin in the morning and Beaudin and his pilots started patroling at 10 A.M. Beaudin said, We stayed up for three to three and a half hours. We then took a half hour break and did another patrol. Sometimes we patrolled till dark." When a fire needed quick attention by the rangers, he could direct them on the radio, right to the fire. "I saw them on the road and I could tell them the best dirt and log roads to take to get to the fire," he says.

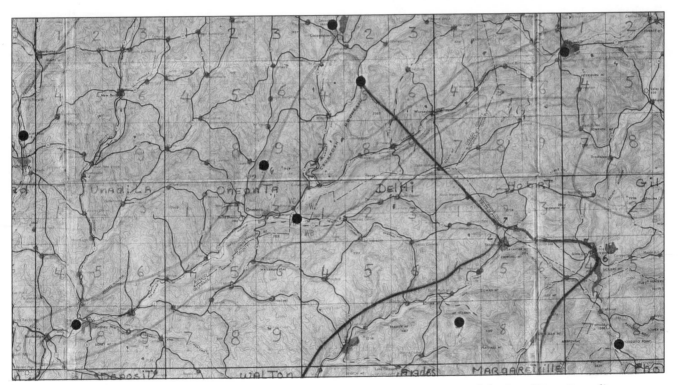

Marcel Thompson flew "1 Bravo," Fred Purdy flew the Oneonta route "Alpha," and Don Beaudin flew the Binghamton route "Charley," the far western route. Marcel Thompson

Notes

1 Louis Curth, *The Forest Rangers*, Albany: N.Y.S. Department of Environmental Conservation, 1987, p. 38.

2 Ibid. pp. 33-34.

3 *Forest, Fish and Game Commission of the State of New York Report 1908,* Albany: J. B. Lyon, State Printers, 1909, p. 34.

4 Ibid. p. 64.

5 Curth, p. 33.

6 Ibid. p 43.

7 *Forest, Fish and Game Commission of the State of New York Report 1908,* Albany: J. B. Lyon, State Printers, 1909, pp. 45-46.

8 Curth, p. 83.

9 Ibid. p. 83.

10 Ibid. pp. 30-31.

11 Ibid. p. 84.

12 *The Third Annual Report of the Conservation Commission 1913,* Albany: 1914, p. 96.

13 *The Conservation Commission Report 1926,* Albany: 1927 p.188.

14 *The Conservation Commission Report 1916,* Albany: 1917 p. 36.

15 *The Conservation Commission Report 1917,* Albany: 1918 p. 69.

16 *The Conservation Commission Report 1919,* Albany: 1920 p. 36.

17 Curth, pp. 89-90

18 *The Conservation Commission Report 1920,* Albany: 1921 pp. 155-157.

19 Curth, p. 85.

20 Ibid. pp. 83-84.

21 *Third Annual Report*, pp. 97-98.

22 *Commission Report 1917*, p. 70.

23 *Commission Report 1919*, pp. 137-138.

24 Ibid. p. 138.

25 The *Conservation Commission Report 1921,* Albany: 1922, p. 124.

26 Curth, p. 45.

27 Ibid. p. 33.

28 *The Conservation Department Report 1927,* Albany: 1928, p.188.

29 *The Conservation Commission Report 1922,* Albany: 1923 p. 165.

30 *Commission Report 1926*, p. 187.

31 Ibid. p. 195.

32 Ibid.

33 Ibid. p. 195-196.

34 *Department Report 1927,* pp. 194.

35 *Commission Report 1922*, p. 166.

36 Gurth Whipple, *Fifty Years of Conservation in New York State 1885-1935,* Albany: N.Y.S. Conservation Department and N.Y.S. College of Forestry, 1935, p. 56.

37 *Commission Report 1921*, pp. 106-108.

38 *Conservation Department Report 1927*, p. 185.

39 *The Conservation Department Report 1932,* Albany: 1933 pp. 86, 88-89.

40 Ibid. p. 89.

41 *The Conservation Department Report 1930,* Albany: 1931, pp. 145-146.

42 Ibid. p. 143.

43 *The Conservation Department Report 1935,* Albany: 1936, p. 26.

44 *The Conservation Department Report 1934,* Albany: 1935, p. 99.

45 *The Conservation Department Report,1931,* Albany: 1932, p. 118.

46 *Department Report 1934* , pp. 99, 101.

47 *The Conservation Department Report 1933,* Albany: 1934, p. 92.

48 *The Conservation Department Report 1938,* Albany: 1939, pp. 92-93, 80-81.

49 *The Conservation Department Report 1938,* Albany: 1939, p. 94.

50 Ibid. p. 130.

51 *The Conservation Department Report 1939,* Albany: 1940, p. 74-75.

52 Ibid. p. 82.

53 *The Conservation Department Report 1944-45,* Albany: 1946, pp. 67-69.

54 Curth, pp. 107, 110.

55 *The Conservation Department Report 1943,* Albany: 1944, pp. 19-20.

56 Ibid. pp. 71-72.

57 *The Conservation Department Report 1948,* Albany: 1949, p. 67.

58 *The Conservation Department Report 1947,* Albany: 1948, pp. 53-54, 56.

59 *The Conservation Department Report 1950,* Albany: 1951, pp. 85, 89.

60 *The Conservation Department Report 1951,* Albany: 1952, pp. 82-83.

61 Ibid. p. 84.

62 Curth, p. 119.

63 Ibid. p. 124.

64 Ibid. pp. 125-127.

65 Curth, p. 124.

66 *The Conservation Department Report 1961,* Albany: 1961, p. 67.

67 Curth, p. 151.

68 Ibid. p. 156.

69 Alf Evers, *The Catskills*, p. 494.

70 Ibid., p. 555.

71 Ibid

72 Ibid., p. 576.

73 *Conservation Commission Annual Report 1912*, p. 27.

74 H. A. Haring, *Our Catskill Mountains*, New York: G. P. Putnam's Sons, 1931.

75 "Slide Mountain," *New York State Conservationist*, Vol. 14 No. 6, June-July 1961.

76 Barbara McMartin and Peter Kick, *Fifty Hikes in the Hudson Valley*, Woodstock, VT: Backcoutry Publications, 1990, p. 125.

77 *Conservation Department Annual Report 1919*, p. 136.

78 *Conservation Department Annual Report 1929*, p. 110.

79 *Conservation Department Annual Report 1935* p.118, *1938* p. 93, *1939* p. 89; *1944-45* p.72; *1947* p.65; *1948* p. 66; *1949* p 70.

Bibliography

Books

Adams, Arthur G., et al. *Guide to the Catskills*. New York: Walking News, Inc., 1975.

Conservation Commission of the State of New York. Annual Reports, 1911-1926.

Conservation Department of the State of New York. Annual Reports, 1927-1965.

Curth, Louis C. *The Forest Rangers: A History of the New York State Forest Ranger Force*. Albany: New York State Department of Environmental Conservation, 1987.

Evers, Alf. *The Catkills: From Wilderness to Woodstock*. Woodstock, N.Y.: The Overlook Press. Reprint of the 1972 Doubleday edition with corrections.

Fagan, Jack. *Scenes and Walks in the Northern Shawangunks*. New York: New York-New Jersey Trail Conference, 1988.

Forest, Fish and Game Commission of the State of New York. Annual Reports, 1900-1910.

Fried, Marc B. *The Huckleberry Pickers: A Raucous History of the Shawangunk Mountains*. Hensonville, N.Y.: Black Dome Press Corp., 1995.

_____ *Shawangunk: Adventure, Exploration, History and Epiphany from a Mountain Wilderness*. Gardiner, N.Y.: published by the author, 1988.

Haring, H. A. *Our Catskill Mountains*. New York: G. P. Putnam's Sons, 1931.

Horton, Gertrude Fitch. *Old Delaware County: A Memoir*. Fleischmanns, N.Y.: Purple Mountain Press, 1993.

Longstreth, T. Morris. *The Catskills*. New York: The Century Co., 1918

Matteson, Benjamin H. "The Story of Sky Top and Its Four Towers." New Paltz: Mohonk Archives booklet, 1996.

McMartin, Barbara and Peter Kick. *Fifty Hikes in the Hudson Valley*. Woodstock, Vermont: Backcountry Publications, 1990.

Studer, Norman. *A Catskill Woodsman: Mike Todd's Story*. Fleischmanns, N.Y.: Purple Mountain Press, 1988.

Tiffany, Lena O. *Pioneers of the Beaverkill Valley*. Published by the author, 1976.

Wadsworth, Bruce. *Guide to Catskill Trails*. Lake George, N.Y.: Adirondack Mountain Club, Inc., 1995.

Reports

New York State Department of Environmental Conservation. "Slide Mountain Wilderness Management Plan." Albany, 1998.

Periodicals

Kaatskill Life. Vol. 8, No. 6, Spring 1993.

New York State Conservationist. Vol. 15, No. 6, June-July 1961. Vol. 39, No. 6, May-June 1985.

Newspapers

The Catskill Mountain News, Margaretville, N.Y.

The Reporter, Walton, N.Y.

Acknowledgments

THANKS to my parents and grandparents who instilled in me the importance of hard work and the value of a good education.

My wife, Lynn, provided support and encouragement throughout the years of research and writing. Thanks to my children, Matthew, Kristy and Ryan, for accompanying me on hikes to the towers. Ryan was the brave soul who climbed the towers and took pictures while his father remained safely below.

Publisher Wray Rominger had faith in my interest in fire towers and gave me the opportunity to write the book.

David Hayden, my editor, has guided me in the writing and rewriting of my stories. Without his encouragement and suggestions, this book would not have been completed.

I am honored Norm Van Valkenburgh wrote the informative foreword to this book.

Thanks to Sallie Way, my sister-in-law, who designed the book cover; to my "adopted" son, Tony Sansavero, who provided the fire tower illustration; to Tony's wife, Maria, who hiked to many of the towers with me; and to Chris Morgan, who drafted the map.

The following faculty and students of Delaware Academy proofread my newspaper articles on fire towers: Pat Corey, Colin MacKenzie, Joanne Patterson, Jennifer Oles and Johanna Outhouse.

Many weekly newspapers in the area published my articles about the towers and the men and women who worked hard to save our Catskill forests. Thanks to the *Delaware County Times* and editor Tim Duerden, who published my first stories. Appreciation is due Parry Teasdale of *Woodstock Times*, who first paid me for my stories. Thanks, also, to editors at *The Walton Reporter*, *The Windam Journal*, *The Mountain Eagle*, *The Sullivan County Democrat*, the Cobelskill *Times Journal*, *The Ellenville Times*, the *Port Jervis Gazette*, the Narrowsburg *River Reporter*.

The wonderful old pictures in the book were loaned to me by many family members of forest rangers and tower observers. Warm thanks to all of you. I would like to acknowledge especially Dot Borden and Betty Baker, who shared their collections of newspaper stories and pictures.

I am grateful for the research material and photographs gathered from the following people and organizations: Jim Ponzio for his *New York State Conservation Report* collection; Pat Christian, Director of Research, Ellenville Public Library and Museum; Paul Huth, Director, Daniel Smiley Research Center; Joan La Chance, Mohonk House Historical Office in New Paltz; and Evelyn Bennett, Curator, Town of Shandaken Historical Museum. Thanks to the Morton Library, Pine Hill; the Cragsmoor Library; the Woodstock Library; the Ogden Free Library, Walton; and the Cannon Free Library, Delhi.

The New York State Department of Environmental Conservation was very helpful in opening up their files to me. A special thanks to Rangers Don Secord and Paul Trotta in Stamford, Pat Kilpeck in Schenectady, Ray Wood in New Paltz, and Tom Rinaldi and Dan Walsh in Albany.

Retired Ranger Ed Hale kindly loaned me his copy of Louis Curth's book, *The Forest Ranger*.

Forest Fire Lookout Association members, especially Fred Knauf, shared their research with me.

Thank you to my good neighbors, Dave and Merry Rama, who provided the equipment for copying materials.

I am grateful to The Roxbury Arts Group, which provided me a New York State Council on the Arts Decentralization Grant through my sponsor, the Bovina Public Library.